My Boy
by
Philomena Lynott
with
Jackie Hayden

Virgin

First published in Great Britain in 1996 by
Virgin Books
an imprint of Virgin Publishing Ltd
332 Ladbroke Grove
LONDON W10 5AH

First published in 1995 by Hot Press Books, 13
Trinity St, Dublin 2

Design by Paula Nolan, Hot Press
Cover Photograph by Denis O'Regan

ISBN 0 7535 0048 5

Printed by Colour Books, Baldoyle Industrial
Estate, Dublin 13

Photographs from Philomena Lynott's personal
collection. Every effort has been made to trace
the copyright holders of the additional photographs in this book but one or two were
unreachable. We would be grateful if the pho-
tographers concerned would contact us.

INTRODUCTION

For an ever-increasing number of music fans spread right across the globe, the name Philip Lynott conjures up images of a hugely successful rock star, at once the Black Irishman vocalist with the unmistakable voice, and a songwriter and musician whose work captured the imagination of millions, and whose songs live on in the hearts of fans everywhere. Those images will also be tinged with the sadness of his personal life and the tragedy of his death.

I hardly need to say that, for me, Philip Lynott was more than just a talented creative artist. He was, above all, a generous and a loving son, with an indomitable spirit and a warm personality who, although he spurned the more ostentatious trappings of wealth, thoroughly enjoyed his glamorous lifestyle, the opportunities it brought him and the characters who peopled it.

The events of his roller-coaster life as a world-famous celebrity were sandwiched between traumatic events, at one end the hardship of his birth and upbringing and, at the other, his wasting away through a drug habit that turned out to be the only serious challenge in his entire life with which he would fail to cope.

My purpose in telling this story, to the best of my ability, is to set the record straight in the face of the many spurious rumours and cheap speculation concerning the circumstances of his birth, life and death that have circulated with increasing degrees of inaccuracy in recent years.

So this book is neither the story of Philip Lynott – Rock Star, nor the sordid tabloid tale of a drug addict. This is my personal story of the affectionate relationship I enjoyed with my only son. It covers the trials and tribulations of a black child born out of wedlock and growing up in a Catholic working-class suburb in the Ireland of the harsh 1950s, his ascent to the dizzy heights of his international rock celebrity and the heart-break of his failed marriage and tragic death.

But above all else, this is a love story . . .

■ PHILOMENA LYNOTT, November 1995

N.B. Some of the names of the people who figure prominently in the early part of my story have been changed in order to protect their privacy.

My Boy

Contents

THE EMIGRANT TRAIL

"How can I leave the town
that brings me down
that has no jobs
is blessed by God
and makes me cry, Dublin."
– from 'Dublin' by Philip Lynott

Growing up in working-class Dublin in the 1940s and '50s involved many similarities with the experiences and prospects of young Irish people in more recent decades. In particular, the threats of joblessness and emigration hung over many of us. At the same time, the influence of the Catholic Church on the society in which I was reared was much deeper than it is today. Indeed, in general, authority, whether that of Church, School, State or parents, expected and received far greater respect than is evident now.

I had been born in a part of the inner city of Dublin known as The Liberties on the 22nd of October 1930, but when I was about four years of age the family moved to Crumlin, a growing working-class suburb further out on the south side of the city. During the often anxious and uncertain years of my childhood, the Irish economy was in a deep depression. Unemployment was high, and the evidence of poverty and squalor on the streets of Dublin was striking. A report published in the *Irish Journal Of Medical Science* in 1932 revealed that one in eight children in the inner-city slums suffered from malnutrition. Diseases such as tuberculosis were rife, claiming hundreds of lives annually.

It is estimated that about 15% of the Irish population of the time took the emigrant boat to England in search of employment. I remember it as a daily fact of life. The Irish newspapers regularly ran advertisements from companies offering not only to pay travel fares from Ireland to England but also offering to arrange jobs and accommodation for those who set off on the emigrant's trail.

I answered one of those ads and not long afterwards a letter arrived confirming that my application had been successful. So I left our cosy family home at 85 Leighlin Road, Crumlin, halfway through 1947, for Birmingham, to stay in a hostel and to train as a nurse.

We had never had any money but I had been happy in Dublin. For a naive seventeen year old, the shock of arriving in what seemed like a whole new world was enormous. I remember thinking, at first, that everything looked different here, even the sky, the clouds and the air so crisp and clean you felt you could almost drink it. Still, I settled down fairly quickly in the strange land to which I had moved and made friends with many other Irish girls from similar backgrounds to my own.

Birmingham was an exciting place in the late 1940s. Vast areas of the largely Victorian city-centre had been decimated by Hitler's World War II bombs, but a campaign of re-building was already underway in earnest. Everywhere you looked, shattered old houses, shops and offices were being salvaged and re-constructed, and foundations for brand new roads and buildings were being laid. Strolling, as I often did, through Brum's many parks and green spaces, I reflected on how lucky I was to be part of this burgeoning sense of a 'fresh start'.

The events that were subsequently to have such a profound bearing on the rest of my life can be traced back to one night in 1949 when one of my friends, Annie Brennan, suggested we go to a dance at a Displaced Persons' Hostel on Wolverhampton New Road in Birmingham. There were similar hostel sites in various parts of England, intended for Poles, Lithuanians and people of other nationalities, mostly displaced from their homelands by the Second World War. They were like army camps, and they often contained a large community centre, a canteen, cinema, church and virtually every other essential amenity. Annie and I began to attend dances regularly in one such hostel. The ballroom was like the old-time dance halls which would be familiar to anyone who remembers the Ireland of the fifties or who saw the film *The Ballroom Of Romance*, where all the ladies stood on one side of the room and the gentlemen on the other, and the music would be provided by a big band.

Such places of entertainment probably attracted Irish girls like Annie and me because they reminded us of home as well as, perhaps, holding out the prospect of meeting a future husband. But, as often happens in these matters, fate had a slightly different plan, for me at least.

Annie and I had been going out to dances at the hostel for about a month during 1948. It wasn't something that I'd have remarked on at the time, but the different nationalities used to keep apart from each other in a casual way, not unlike the tradition in Irish dance-halls. But when the music struck up, such differences were usually put aside and we danced the night away, mixing perfectly naturally with each other and with a great sense of fun.

Two Polish boys took a shine to Annie and me and often danced with us. My Polish friend was called Janek. Apart from enjoying lots of dancing with them, they also took us one night to see the film *Forever Amber*. Whenever I see that film on television, it brings back memories of those seemingly far-off days during which Janek and I dated for about two months in spite of the fact that he, like many of his fellow countrymen in England at that time, had very little English. In fact, he grew rather fond of me to the extent that I think he regarded me as his girl-friend and wanted to have every dance with me.

One night when we were all in the dance-hall, a tall black gentleman walked across the dance-floor and invited me to dance. His name was Cecil Parris. Little did I know it then, but he was to become the father of my one and only son, Philip. When we finished our first dance, which had three encores, I walked back to where I had been standing. I remember vividly that all the other ladies moved away from me. I heard somebody angrily mutter "nigger-lover" within my earshot. That was my first encounter with any kind of racial intolerance, and it shocked and upset me.

I had grown up totally unaware of such racial prejudice. Black people were a rarity in Dublin, apart from those one would see in the movies, or the occasional black students I might have observed around Trinity College, when I travelled into the centre of Dublin with my school friends or on an errand for my mother. So I could not understand what was supposed to be so dreadfully wrong in dancing with a black man, or why anyone should have started calling me horrible names because I had done so. Indeed, how could I have refused a man who had walked the length of the dance floor to ask me to dance? In my eyes, to do so would have been an act of extreme rudeness. Besides, I thought, that's what ladies went to dances for, to be invited to dance! I could never, and would never, refuse to dance with any man who politely asked me. There might have been times when I did not like the appearance of a guy who invited me to dance, but I would not hurt any individual by rejecting him so openly in a public place.

There were probably only about a dozen black men out of a fairly packed attendance at that dance, and I could not help noticing how they tended to gather together in one part of the hall, much like the other ethnic groups and nationalities. Of course when I agreed to dance with this man, I didn't even know his name or anything about him. I was simply hoping for a pleasant dance, nothing more, nothing less. And so it turned out, that night.

Unfortunately, my Polish friend Janek did not see things quite so simply. As Annie and I made our way out of the hall, we were confronted by

Janek and his Polish buddy, both of whom were showing the effects of having had too much to drink. They both started to rough me up because I had been dancing with Cecil. Their aggression frightened me, but when I tried to run away they grabbed me and forced me up against a wall. By this point I was really terrified and did not know what might happen to me until, from the darkness, I heard a stern voice telling them to let me go. It was Cecil who had seen what was going on. As soon as Janek and his cowardly friend saw that Cecil meant business, they threw me on the ground and ran off into the night. I cannot describe how relieved I was to have been rescued from what was a thoroughly frightening experience.

Determined not to let such boorish behaviour stop us enjoying ourselves, Annie and I attended that same dance-hall several times, and on nearly every occasion, I danced with the same friendly black man. He was handsome as well as tall and I was gradually getting to like him more. Then, one night, he asked me for a date, and took me to a different dance-hall. For about three months, we did what was called 'courting' in the 1940s and 1950s, and spent a lot of time in each other's company in and around Birmingham. But whenever we were seen together in a public place, people would stare at us since a black man and a white woman together was an unusual sight in those days.

Over a period of time, our relationship blossomed as we discovered we really liked one another and a close, reasonably serious relationship developed. Then, one sunny day, we made love. For me, it was the very first time in my life, and it happened on a local golf course. Our sexual relationship continued intermittently for a while. However, within a matter of weeks, Cecil informed me that he was being transferred down to London because of his work in the services, but he promised to keep in touch. Shortly afterwards, I was horrified to discover that I was pregnant. It was as strange and as simple as that.

By some remarkable coincidence, my Irish girlfriend Annie told me that she had missed her period and she thought she too must be pregnant. I suppose we were equally alarmed by our plight, alone in a strange country, expecting babies out of wedlock against all the teachings of our Irish Catholic upbringing. We didn't know what to do and didn't feel that we had anyone we could turn to. It was a popular belief at the time – a superstition I suppose – that if a pregnant woman drank boiled gin with some pennies in it, her periods would return and the pregnancy would miraculously disappear. The only thing was that you had to act during the first month of your pregnancy! So Annie and I furtively gathered together a miniature bottle of gin, a bundle of wood, a discarded bean-can and some newspapers and took them to a field. We dug a shallow hole in the ground in which to burn the wood to heat the gin in a billy-can we had borrowed from the hostel canteen.

As I neither smoked nor drank at the time, I had no previous experience of alcohol. Annie swallowed hers without difficulty, but when I raised mine to my mouth, the smell of it made me retch. Thus ended my first amateurish attempt at aborting my pregnancy! Then someone told us that quinine tablets, which were often used to alleviate malaria, would bring back our periods. We tried that method too, but all I got was a severe headache. Gradually, it sank in that I would have to accept the fact that none of these tricks would work. I suppose I also began to understand what was really happening to me – and to accept it. Apart from that naive, failed attempt, I did not for a moment consider any other means of aborting my pregnancy. It's not that I'm against abortion. I have always believed in a woman's right to choose, but for me to go on and have the baby was definitely the right decision – I was never in any doubt about that, despite the terrible treatment I would be subjected to along the way.

After four months, my pregnancy really began to become obvious, and a source of intense whispering in the hostel where I was staying. When my secret was exposed, I was ruthlessly expelled and my career as a nurse abruptly ended before it had even begun. So much for the ethics of the caring profession at the time.

Fortunately, Birmingham, the second largest city in England, was in those days a thriving industrial capital in which work was comparatively widely available. Scores of famous British business names had their roots in Brum, from Cadbury chocolates, HP sauce and Typhoo tea to breweries such as Davenports, Ansells, and Mitchells and Butlers. The biggest employers of all, though, were Dunlop tyres, and the vast Austin Motor Company.

Established by Herbert Austin in 1906, in Birmingham's Longbridge area, Austin Motors was one of the world's first mass-production car factories. In the post-war years, it was to become one of the most successful companies in Britain. And, it was in the Austin Motors foundry that I managed to find a job, at piece-work rates. Conditions at the foundry were primitive and the foremen were all ferocious taskmasters, their minds set on nothing but meeting the crushing weekly quota figures. It was strenuous and often dirty work for a lonely young girl, unmarried and four months into an unplanned pregnancy. Every evening, as I clocked out, exhausted, grimy and weak from the day's efforts, I would stare at the beautiful pastoral countryside of the Lickey Hills which rose up behind the foundry, and wonder despondently what was to become of me and my unborn child. However, I continued working at Austin Motors right up to the week before my baby was born, struggling to disguise my swollen shape by holding my tummy in and wearing a tight corset.

Meanwhile, I had had to find a place to stay. It wasn't easy, but eventually a childless married woman called Mrs Beardsley, who was crippled with a very bad leg, gave me a bedroom to share with another Irish girl – who, incidentally, is still alive and living in Liverpool.

At the time, I was rather fond of knitting and I produced many items of clothing for my baby over those months, as well as a jumper and some white socks for Mr Beardsley because he was a keen cricket fan. When I think about it now, it all seems so innocent. The couple seemed to have taken a liking to me and were very kind, although they knew that I had not had the courage to inform my parents in Dublin about the secret I was still trying to conceal from the world.

The Beardsleys promised that when my baby was born, we could both return to live with them and they kindly offered to take care of my baby if I later chose to return to work. Even today, over forty years on, I carry a precise picture of their house, and its pleasant surroundings, in my mind. It is amazing the impact that kindness and generosity can have on a lonely and vulnerable girl in a time of crisis. But it was not to last.

As nature took its course, there came a day when I began to feel a little strange and was taken by ambulance to Halham Hospital, in the West Bromwich part of Birmingham, where I was eventually to endure a full 36 hours in labour. The nurses knew that my baby was illegitimate and I was convinced that this knowledge gave some of them delusions of superiority over me. I walked around a lot trying to ease my labour pains until one of them forced me to drink a cup of thick, unpleasant, castor oil. She said it would make the baby come quicker, but I suspected that she was just being cruel.

I heard some mothers screaming, 'Oh, I'll never forgive you, oh, I'll never forgive you! Never again', and so on during their deliveries, but I never once called out. I bore my son proudly despite experiencing the most intense labour pains, and I did not wince or cry out. I remember grabbing the iron bars of the bed with white-knuckled ferocity and holding on for dear life. I was aware of the nurses gathered around me, perhaps waiting for a glimpse at the comparative novelty of an unmarried Irish woman bringing a black child into the world, but I didn't care. They wouldn't intimidate or upset me. Such was their curiosity that some of them even took pictures of us!

My son was born on 20th August 1949. He weighed nine and a half pounds and was twenty-one and a half inches long at birth. Only another mother will fully comprehend the overwhelming feeling of elation and the sense of wonder I felt at first seeing and holding my beautiful new baby, the difficult circumstances of his birth and our uncertain future temporarily banished from my mind. After the birth, I was put in a ward with six beds. I can recall that room to this day, with the babies' cots standing at the foot of the beds during visiting hours, while at all other times they were kept in a separate nursery.

I named him Philip Parris Lynott. I chose the name Philip because during my mother Sarah's pregnancy with me, my father Frank became very ill. My mother prayed to St. Philomena, promising that if Frank regained his strength she would call her baby Philomena, or the male equivalent, Philip, in the case of a boy. Shortly before I was born, my father began to enjoy his full health again and that's how I became Philomena, or Phyllis for short.

When it came to my turn to be a mother, I remembered that story. Throughout my life, I had often prayed to St. Philomena and it had seemed to me that she regularly eased my troubles. So it really disappointed me years later, in 1961, when it was officially announced by Rome that there had been no such person as St. Philomena, and that the feast of St. Philomena, on August 11th, was to be discontinued.

For Philip's second name, I chose Parris after his father, Cecil Parris. The horrible thing was that throughout my trauma, Philip's father was still unaware of my situation. He had written from London to me at the hostel, but because I had been evicted, none of his letters was forwarded to me. When visitors came to see the other women with their babies, I used to bury my head and cry, wondering what would become of my beautiful, innocent, little baby and me. I had no visitors. The Beardsleys never came and I envied the other mothers who all received regular visits from husbands, family and friends.

But difficult though my plight was, it was as nothing compared to the experience of one lady there, who had unfortunately lost her baby at birth. A couple of days after Philip was born, her relations called to take her home early. Understandably, she could not bear to remain in the same ward as us, with our healthy babies. As she was waving good-bye to me, her own mother handed me about four boxes containing all the clothes which had been bought for the dead baby. That was the first act of genuine kindness shown to me since becoming a mother and it came from a total stranger.

About four days later, the matron came to me and casually dropped a bombshell. "Philomena," she said," you have nowhere to go when you leave here. Your landlady has sent us all your bits and pieces in a suitcase, so we have to make arrangements to place you in a home."

This news really hurt me desperately. My landlady and her husband had promised to visit the hospital, and I had been deeply disappointed when they had not done so. But now I discovered that, unknown to me, they had arrived at the hospital, had been shown Philip in the nursery and had walked straight out again on seeing that he was black. They returned to their house immediately, packed up all my belongings and delivered them to the matron who was now, without any forewarning or any hint of Christian sympathy, giving me the dreadful news that I was bound for a home for unmarried mothers.

I had never heard of the Selly Oak Home For Unmarried Mothers before. It was located amid the lush daffodil and tulip beds of the Selly Oak suburb in Birmingham. I was taken there with my baby in my arms. It was a beautiful old mansion-type building set among vast grounds, with a small chapel visible at the end of the gardens. There was also a very old Victorian outhouse – the purpose of which I discovered later.

I was allotted a bed in a dormitory with several other young mothers, while Philip was put in a nursery full of babies in cots, arranged in neat rows. The Mother Superior sternly informed me that, as long as I was staying there, I would have to work to earn my keep. The jobs for the girls included keeping the dormitories clean, looking after the nurseries, polishing the dining room and assisting the cook. Having spent so long working in a car foundry, to me these seemed like potentially pleasant tasks by comparison.

The Victorian outhouse turned out to be the laundry and, unfortunately, I was put to work there. To reach it, you had to leave the big warm house, walk across the yard and enter this old, unfriendly building with its cold, stone floor. It was fitted with large sinks, or troughs as they were called, and in the corner stood an enormous drum full of water and a gas heater to boil it. The drum had a big stick in it for pounding the clothes up and down. One of the sinks was used only for dirty nappies. This was long before the days of the disposable nappy and I had to stand in that laundry for hours on end and let the water wash the smelly dirt from each nappy into a sluice before putting it into a second sink to be rinsed, and then into the big boiler.

They had clearly given me the toughest job going and I believed this was a deliberate form of punishment, not only for having an illegitimate child, but perhaps more especially on account of the fact that he was black. Maybe that's being paranoid, but I certainly could sense that they looked down on me, and most of them clearly did not even want to talk to me, including some of the nuns.

Every weekend, the mothers were ordered to make their babies look pretty and all the cots would be set out on the lawn. Visitors, strangers to us all, would parade around peering closely at our babies in their cots. This activity puzzled me. I did not understand who these people were or what they were doing, and I became particularly intrigued whenever I saw them standing over Philip's cot, staring intently at my baby, who always looked gorgeous in the blue clothes I had knitted. One day, I asked one of the other mothers, a tough young girl named Mary, to explain what this was all about. "Don't you know?" she said, "they've come to adopt the babies. The day your baby is adopted, that's the day you get out of this prison."

I was astonished at this. Indignantly, I said: "I'm not giving my baby up for adoption," but she repeated the same refrain. "I'm telling you, that's the only way you'll get out of here," she insisted. I was distraught at the very idea of losing my beautiful baby boy. If there was anything I could do to prevent it, I would.

Next day, I met Mary again. She asked me, "How old are you?" I told her I would be eighteen before too long. "Oh, you'll be all right then," she said casually. "They can't take your baby from you when you're eighteen." I thought it extraordinary, and extremely cruel, that nobody had even bothered to tell me what was going on. I also realised that, in sharp contrast to my own feelings of protectiveness towards my baby, Mary actually wanted hers adopted so that she could quit the home and continue her life as before.

She was not alone. There was a Polish girl in the home called Maria with a baby called Johnny. I'll never forget him. He was as blonde as the driven snow, with lovely blue eyes but with an unusually enlarged head. Mary pointed at Maria one day. "See her?" she said. "She can't wait to have her baby adopted so she can get back to her boyfriend." Maria had managed to maintain contact with the father of the baby because we were allowed out one afternoon each week, to walk to the nearby village of Selly Oak. I could not understand how she could be so casual about something as important as her baby, although Mary reckoned that Maria was going to be in the home a long time, because, as she callously believed, nobody would want to adopt a baby with an abnormal head.

While having my bath one night in the ground floor bathroom close to the laundry, I left the window open to let the steam out, and I was shocked to hear Maria loudly arguing. "No, no, I'm not doing that job," she said. "Let the mother of the nigger do it." Her cruel and ignorant words echo in my mind because it was the first time I had heard my baby referred to as a nigger.

I remember leaping angrily out of the bath. I probably didn't even stop to dry off. In my anger, I hurried across to the laundry where I found Maria with one of the nuns, of whom she seemed to be a particular favourite, and I furiously launched myself at her. "Don't you dare call my baby a nigger!" I roared. She abused me in turn and left no doubt about how much she despised any mother who would give birth to a black baby. It was a terrible scene but I was so upset that I couldn't help myself. I continued swinging at her while the nun struggled to restrain me, but I broke free, grabbed the pounding stick from the drum and swung it at the pair of them in such a wild temper that others heard the commotion, rushed in and forced me down.

I was then instructed to go to the chapel, to ask God to forgive me. So I was marched to the chapel. There I stood before the altar screaming at them: "What am I asking forgiveness for? Why are they calling my baby a nigger?" I was in complete emotional turmoil and was totally distraught at the injustice of the situation. I couldn't understand why they were treating me like this. I calmed down eventually but, in the days that followed, I wondered if life for me and my Philip was always going to be fraught with such pain.

One day soon afterwards, the Matron ordered me to report to the Committee Room, which was furnished with a table so beautifully polished that, whenever the nuns in their habits were seated around it, you could see their faces clearly reflected in the furiously waxed surface. When I entered the room, the Mother Superior was already seated, with two nuns and a priest from Selly Oak village church and a sheaf of official-looking documents spread out before them.

After ordering me to sit down, one of them said: "Philomena, we are making arrangements to send you back to Ireland to start a new life and we have some good news for you. We have found a married couple who are willing to adopt Philip." This was all put to me with a great sense of authority and it was emphasised that they knew how good this move would be for me. If they had had their way, I would have been given absolutely no say in the deliberations. But I wasn't going to let them take my child away from me.

"Just a minute," I said. "This is my baby and I'm not parting with him." With that, I fled from the room, ran upstairs, grabbed Philip and locked us both inside the nursery. It may sound melodramatic now, but at the time I was in desperation. That led to much pounding on the door. Apart from anything else, I think they were concerned that I might be going to harm myself or Philip, which was not my intention at all. Eventually, and after much negotiation, I agreed to come out. They seemed to have realised the extent of my determination not to allow anyone to separate us, because they then threatened to inform my parents in Dublin. Of course, nobody in Ireland yet knew anything about me having had a baby. My family was a conventionally respectable Catholic Irish family. My father had proudly walked my older sisters down the aisle on their wedding days. I was, as it were, the 'wild' one, and I had been terrified that they would hear of my predicament.

I was presented with a simple but cruel choice, bordering on blackmail. Unless I was prepared to surrender Philip for adoption, the home no longer wanted me, and they would have to pass me and Philip over to whoever would then be legally responsible for us. Cecil was still unaware of Philip's existence. Because I had been dumped out of my digs, I received none of his letters, although whenever I bumped into anyone who might have news of him, they would tell me that he had been enquiring about me. Without him, I was in a real quandary.

A photographer called regularly to the home to take pictures of the babies and any mother who so desired could be photographed with her baby. Though I didn't realise it at the time, those photos were intended to be shown to potential adoptive parents. My photo had been taken with Philip, but it would now be used for a different purpose. I was forced to write informing my mother in Crumlin that I had a baby, and that I did not know where the father was. From what I can remember, the letter simply went, "Dear Mummy, I'm enclosing a photograph of me with a little baby, and the little baby is my son and he's three months old."

I later found out that when my mother opened the envelope she looked at the picture and initially thought, "What a lovely little black baby with our Phyllis." But when she read the letter through and realised the reality of my position, she collapsed.

I suppose most Irish mothers would have reacted similarly at the time, faced with a revelation of this kind. It may be difficult now for people to

24

understand the social pressures prevalent in the Dublin of the early 1950s compared to the liberalism of today, but to my mother this news was a tremendous shock that went against all her religious beliefs and her expectations for her daughters. At the same time, she was very good about it. When she had recovered and talked things over with my father, she despatched my brother John to England to meet me. As he was obviously from a respectable background, his arrival at least proved to the nuns in the Home that I came from a caring family. I was again summoned to the Committee Room, so that arrangements could be made for my brother to take me back to the family home in Crumlin. But I was convinced that the family, including my brother John, had already decided to bring me back merely in order to persuade me to let Philip go for adoption and I adamantly refused to co-operate in this new plan. I had been through such emotional upheaval that I didn't know who I could trust. I was full of fear and paranoia, as well as an inevitable sense of loneliness and isolation at being separated from the father of my little baby.

At yet another meeting in the Committee Room, John, who was himself about to get married, again attempted to persuade me but I insisted, "no, no, no." I can still remember the look in his eyes as he said goodbye before returning to Crumlin, obviously feeling so sorry for me, both because of my situation and because I was stubbornly making life even more difficult for myself.

Shortly afterwards, the Home authorities delivered me an ultimatum. If I found a place for Philip and me to live, we would be permitted to leave, but since I would not have my baby adopted I could not stay indefinitely in what, they kept reminding me, was a respectable Catholic home. Irrespective of any threats or schemes, I was more determined than ever to keep my baby, no matter what difficulties or obstacles might lie in waiting for us. But I still felt terribly isolated and alone.

MY GUARDIAN ANGEL

Totally out of the blue, a knock came to the door of my dormitory at the Home and the Mother Superior informed me that a man had arrived claiming to be the father of my baby. It was Cecil and, as we held each other for the first time in many months, we both broke down in tears. "Why didn't you find some way to tell me about all this?" he asked me, through his sobs, and I explained that I had no way of contacting him in my lonely, confused state. But I was so relieved to finally have at least one sympathetic person to talk to. I told him about everything that had happened to me and Philip since I had last met him. When he had absorbed my full story, he promised to find a place, or digs as they were called, for us.

To his eternal credit, despite the fact that winter was coming on and the weather was awful, he went out searching for somewhere for us to live. Unfortunately, the evils of racial prejudice were rooted far deeper in English society than I could possibly have imagined and, try as he might, nobody wanted us. Much later, the fellow who was the singer with the Sex Pistols, John Lydon, wrote a book about his life called *No Irish, No Blacks, No Dogs*. Well, I know only too well what he was talking about. Those were the offensive words used on signs frequently placed in the windows of houses with vacancies. But, more often, an unwritten, unspoken but deeply ingrained attitude based on ignorance and fear, prevailed.

Eventually, after much heartache and many point-blank refusals, he found a Mrs. Cavendish with a house in the working-class suburb of Blackheath, Birmingham, who said she would take me into her house on condition I agreed to share a double-bed with her teenage daughter,

Dorothy. Cecil would not be staying with us because of his work in London, but he would be allowed to visit fairly frequently and I would be permitted to keep Philip's cot with me in the bedroom. Of course, when the Social Welfare people came to inspect our living quarters, Mrs Cavendish said nothing about the bed-sharing arrangement. The inspectors found a nice clean house, approved of the situation and gave us the all-clear to move in.

As it turned out, there were further indignities to come. After my first night under a new roof, I awoke to find that Dorothy, with whom I had been told to share the bed and who was about the same age as myself, had wet the bed and urinated all over me. I realised that she must have a slight mental problem. But as this was the only half-decent place Cecil could find for us after trudging all over Birmingham for weeks, I had to be thankful that we were at least free of all the unpleasantness of the dreadful Home.

And there were other compensations. Edith, the second daughter in the house, became a really close friend to me and after I was only about two months there, she confided that she too was pregnant. The first question I asked her was, "Does your Mother know?" She said, "No," and then she said, "The baby's going to be black and I can't stay here much longer. I'm going to have to run away."

It then emerged that Cecil had been able to arrange these digs because he was acquainted with the black man who was the father of Edith's baby. Ironically, but for that coincidence, there might have been no escape for me and Philip from the Home. Who knows what fate might otherwise have overtaken us?

I had already decided that I would have to try to earn some money, even though Cecil was sending me as much as he could towards Philip's upkeep. After several attempts, I secured yet another job amid the noise, grime and back-breaking quotas of my old friend, the Austin Motor Company. In order to be on time for work in Longbridge, which was on the other side of Birmingham, in time, I left the house at six-thirty every morning to travel in a type of motor-bus called a charabanc. I would arrive home after a heavy day's work as late as seven-thirty in the evening.

Mrs Cavendish had agreed to mind Philip while I was at work in return for payment, but the arrangement never really worked satisfactorily. The long trek to and from work, and the hard working day, were enough to drain all my energies. As you can imagine, it used to anger me greatly to arrive home most evenings to find Philip still wearing the same nappy I had put on him before leaving early that morning. It was obvious that she had not even bothered to attend to such a basic chore, even though she was charging me a lot of money for minding him and for my digs, in which I had, after all, to share a bed. Every night, after a hard day's work I would have to spend ages washing Philip and his clothes. Needless to say, I was disgusted at the way we were being treated.

But when I recalled with horror all the indignities I had endured at the Home, as well as the extreme difficulties Cecil had experienced in getting us even this meagre accommodation, I realised I had no alternative but to persevere. I could at least draw some consolation from having Philip with me, and with my wages and the occasional contribution from Cecil, we were able to get by despite the problems.

Unfortunately, this comparative security was not to last for long. While standing in a queue one day at a local fish and chip shop, another neighbour asked me, "Don't you live around the corner with Mrs Cavendish?" I confirmed that I did. Then she said, "Haven't I seen you wearing a lovely maroon-coloured coat?" She was referring to a beautiful coat Cecil had given me as a Christmas present around the time that I left the Home. I said "Yes, you probably have." Then she continued, "Well I often see that landlady of yours wearing it when she goes out to the pub."

It finally dawned on me the extent to which my precious baby was being cruelly neglected by the very woman who was actually being paid to mind him. I knew I could not tolerate this situation much longer, so I asked Edith when she was planning to move away. When she said, "As soon as possible," we agreed to run away together to Manchester.

On reading about my experiences, some people may, understandably I suppose, suspect that I just had a little too much to drink one night, met a man, had sex and became pregnant. Others may even presume that I was promiscuous and that I was just one of those who get caught. But the truth is somewhat different and far less dramatic. In reality I had simply been enjoying a genuine, very loving relationship with a man for the first time in my life. We cared about each other very dearly and our relationship was such that I even corresponded with Cecil's mother and sisters for a time. And, in the same way, the reason our relationship eventually ended is not particularly earth-shattering.

Cecil's reputation for his good clothes sense had earned him the nickname 'The Duke'. While I was in the digs in Blackheath, he used to travel up from London sometimes to take me to a dance, while my landlord's daughter Edith looked after Philip. During one dance, I visited the powder room and overheard two girls discussing a man. One of them said, "Did you see The Duke with a new girl tonight? He took me home the other night." Or words to that effect. I was devastated. I realised that, in spite of all I had been through, he was carrying-on with other girls behind my back. I suppose I was naive to assume that I was the only one he was seeing – but that was what I had believed. The prolonged separations which circumstances had imposed on us obviously hadn't helped, but I couldn't stand the thought that he had been two-timing me. Our relationship had lasted for about two years – but after much heart-searching, just before Edith and I resolved to abscond to Manchester, I decided there was no long-term future in a relationship with a man I could no longer trust.

Since I had first discovered my pregnancy, there had been many times when I was almost overcome with anxiety. The fact that the majority of my family were far away in Dublin meant that I was often prey to loneliness and insecurity. I had two older sisters living in Leeds, but only one of these, Monica, kept in regular contact with me. She knew about Philip and felt sympathy for me, particularly after I had written to Mammy with news which, predictably, had resulted in few people wanting to know me.

Everywhere I turned, I was reminded of the extent to which an Irish girl with a black baby was a social outcast. Monica was married and while she was expecting her own baby I asked if I could visit her and take Philip with me. She agreed, but after she met us off the train at Leeds station we had to walk around until darkness fell, in order to make sure that her land-lady didn't see her bringing a black baby into the house.

It was that kind of awful, mean-spirited world then, where anything unconventional was frowned upon and people were made to feel guilty about the most natural and innocent things.

Monica arranged for me to sleep on the settee in her small flat that night. It sounds crazy looking back from this vantage point, but every time Philip cried we were terrified in case the landlady would become aware of Philip's illicit presence in the house. Unfortunately, the landlady did eventually hear him and promptly came to investigate. When she saw Philip, she was determined to throw both of us into the street in the mid-dle of the night, but after much pleading she relented and allowed us stay until morning. I cried once again, because of the unfair way I and my innocent baby were being treated. It was heartbreaking – but at least I knew that in my sister Monica I had found someone who was not too far away and who cared about us in a way that was very genuine. At a time when I most needed some kindness and charity, these were very rare commodities indeed.

After fleeing from Blackheath, Edith and I arrived by train in Manchester. An energetic industrial city, then encircled by an enormous ring of active collieries, Manchester is, as I was to learn, a place of many faces, from the conspicuously ritzy to the dreadfully impoverished. To the outsider, however, it can be a cold, unwelcoming landscape, its air of rush and bustle serving only to alienate anyone who does not already have a secure foothold within the life of the city.

All of a sudden, therefore, I now found myself in what I took to be a strange and ugly world with ramshackle houses and foul back-alleys everywhere, and not a tree or a flower to be seen. I was genuinely frightened by the bleak and forbidding atmosphere of our new surroundings, but there was little time to dwell on my fear. Our first priority in this unfamiliar city was to find somewhere to stay. From previous bitter experience, I knew that our only chance would be in the poorer districts, where a woman with a black baby would be more easily accepted.

Finally, after much searching, we found a place with an African landlord who gave us a room and, in the beginning at least, was generally very kind to us. At this point, we had cut ourselves adrift from virtually everybody. None of our friends or family knew where we were, with the exception of the father of Edith's baby because she had written to him. In a sense, we were two girls alone – with one baby to take care of and another one on the way – against the world.

To help us get by, Edith and I came to an arrangement whereby I would go out to work to earn enough money to keep all three of us, leaving her free to concentrate on taking care of Philip and looking after herself as her own pregnancy developed. Out of necessity, we had postponed fretting about the long-term future until after her baby was born. That said, we were not so naive as to imagine that there was anything other than stormy waters up ahead. We encountered them sooner than anticipated.

Our lodgings contained a cellar which had been converted into a kitchen. Because of her growing pregnancy, Edith found it increasingly difficult to make it down the steps, so it fell to me to do all the trips to the cellar to cook and to put pennies in the meter. My weight had dropped down to about seven stone by this time. I was as skinny as a rake. But there's something in the human spirit that makes it hard to crush, and in spite of all the difficulties and anxieties we were managing to get by quite merrily. Then, an unexpected problem raised its ugly head. Many women have had this experience. I know that I'm not at all unique but that doesn't make the memory any more palatable.

One night, I was in the cellar cooking dinner and the landlord, who up until then had behaved very well towards us all, started fondling me. I told him, "No, no, no, go away," and after much struggling I finally shook him off. Edith and I were both disgusted by his behaviour, but we hoped he had got the message and that there would be no repeat of his overbearing approaches. Then, another night soon afterwards, without any warning, in the small hours, he started beating on our door demanding to be allowed into the room we shared. We were so terrified that I ran out and went straight to the nearby police station and screamed at them that our landlord was getting heavy with us. They immediately despatched a policeman to accompany me back to our lodgings, but when he saw Philip in his cot he assumed the black landlord was Philip's father and adopted an extremely unsympathetic attitude towards me, eventually abandoning us altogether to sort out what he obviously interpreted as a family squabble.

When I think about it now, it was absolutely disgraceful – there's no knowing what our presumptuous landlord friend might have done to us, given that I had already gone to the police. As luck would have it, an Irish lady living across the road from our lodgings had heard the commotion with Edith and me screaming and she had observed the policeman entering the house. Seeing how upset we were, and perhaps realising that the police were totally unconcerned, she invited us, there and then, in the middle of the night, to move into her house temporarily.

The following day, Edith decided that she was unable to tolerate any more abuse and uncertainty, and she opted to return to her parents in Blackheath. To be honest, I didn't blame her – but there I was, left alone with Philip at yet another new address.

In due course, the Irish woman, who was genuinely helpful, told me about a Mrs. Freeman who owned a night-club in Manchester and who needed what was then referred to as a skivvy – someone to do household chores for her. I went to see her. Mrs. Freeman advised me that she would provide Philip and me with board and lodgings. In return, I had to take care of her three children, thus leaving her free to run the nightclub. It seemed like a decent, straightforward arrangement. My main responsibilities were to keep the house clean, take her children to and from school, feed them, dress them and so on. So once again we found ourselves living under a different roof.

In retrospect, I suppose this was my first real contact with the entertainment business, with which such a large proportion of my future was to be taken up. It turned out to be a tough job. I had to work morning, noon and night, scrubbing and cleaning the front doorsteps, taking care of the shopping, bringing the kids to the pictures, and giving Mrs. Freeman and her black African husband their breakfast in bed. It was a hard life, but at least the fact that we both had children by black men gave us something in common, and there was no fear of anyone in the house being prejudiced against Philip because of the colour of his skin. And besides, a lot of people had to work extremely hard to get by in the 1950s. They were hard times all 'round.

As you can imagine, I was far too busy simply surviving even to think of starting a relationship, platonic or otherwise, with any man. Friendships of that kind could not have been further from my thoughts, not because I had developed any dislike of, or grudge against, men but simply because I was physically and mentally exhausted working daily from dawn till dusk. I know that I could begin to sound like a perpetual moaner talking like this, but I do think that I was taken advantage of. For while I had comfortable lodgings, my new boss virtually enslaved me. At the end of each gruelling day, all I was fit for was sleeping and cuddling Philip. Every ounce of energy was drained from me by a woman whom I gradually perceived to be tyrannical and heartless.

Having grown up in Ireland in the bosom of a close family, as what people would probably describe as a 'good Catholic girl', I was totally bewildered by the turmoil that had overtaken me and the absence of any signs of friendship in the alien and difficult existence I was forced to lead in order to keep my son. There was not a soul I could turn to, yet not for a second did I entertain the thought of giving in. I was fiercely determined to overcome all these trials, particularly after all the hurt and abuse we had suffered to date, and to allow nothing or nobody to get the better of us. I'd look at little Philip and shudder as I asked myself, "What if I never saw him again?" I was young and naive and didn't have any idea what was involved in bringing up a child, but he was all that mattered to me. Without him, I would be nothing and life would not be worth living. I know I was confused but in my heart of hearts that was how I felt.

Although some people have since asked me where I drew my strength from, I have never really seen myself in any kind of heroic light. When my own mother had babies, and she had five more after I was born, I had helped nurse them from their earliest days. Mammy would say, "You walk him up and down, Phyllis, and make him tired while I do the washing." I had a lot of responsibility thrust upon me from a very early age, so when I had my own baby, I instinctively felt I could love him and care for him as much as any mother.

Of course, some people will say that the father should have been there to share that responsibility, and ideally he would, but in fairness to Cecil, it was I who had broken off the relationship. Now I was as determined as ever to make a life for Philip and myself away from him. Of course, I was not so stupid as to imagine that we would have an easy passage through life. Mrs. Freeman, my latest "employer", did not even pay me wages. She found it cheaper to turn a blind eye to me drawing the dole and receiving child allowance. I was useful to her as a skivvy and she would pretend to the social security people that I rented my room. In a sense she enslaved me at the expense of the State and I was too young and too insecure to break free.

Despite the fact that I felt badly exploited, there was no point in complaining since I had no real alternative. And, deep down, I have to admit that, in some ways, I was reasonably happy with the situation, all things considered. Philip had the other children to play with, and sometimes I would take them all to the cinema, where seats, I remember, cost four old pence each. That was our only weekend treat, but we were well fed, we had a comfortable room and I often had to remind myself that there were many other people enduring far more austere conditions than ours.

One night, a taxi called to the house after the children had gone to bed. The driver told me "Your boss wants you to leave the children asleep and come over to the night-club straightaway." On arriving at the club, she put me behind the bar where, without any prior warning or discussion, washing glasses became yet another of my regular duties. I suppose that was another way in which people's respect for authority worked. I did what I was told. Again, I didn't feel that I had any other option.

While working at the bar one night soon afterwards, I felt someone staring intently at me. When I looked up, I saw a black GI who was drinking on his own. American soldiers were not an uncommon sight in Britain in those days as the U.S. Army still had numerous bases located throughout the country. But this particular one made a big impression. And it was obvious that he couldn't take his eyes off me either. This scene was repeated over several nights, the same dark eyes fixed on me as I worked behind the busy bar. After the taxi had delivered me back to the house one particular night, and just as I was putting the key in the door, a voice behind me said, "Excuse me." When I turned around, it was the same GI. "Can I have a word with you?" he asked.

I remember that he was quite polite, but I was still terribly apprehensive. I curtly asked him what he wanted.

"What's the deal with you?" he said. "Every night they bring you to the club to wash glasses and then you're brought straight back to this house. It doesn't make sense." My initial response was to feel that he was putting my work and my security at risk.

"I can't talk to you, and if they catch you here you'll get me thrown out," I told him. "I've got a little baby and he's black, and I can't afford to risk losing my lodgings by being seen talking to you." Or words to that effect.

"I'll go now, but I'll be back," he said, and he got into a car and drove off. The following night, he reappeared at the club and slipped a note to me asking me to telephone him. When I rang him the next day, he asked me what my story was.

"How did you get into this situation? Tell me everything," he insisted. I had no idea what he really wanted but I suppose it's nice to be able to pour out your troubles, so I told him my story from start to finish.

He listened intently, which made me feel good. When I finished, he said: "Why don't you let me take care of you?"

It was the last thing I expected to hear. I remember feeling that nobody wants to know me, so why should he? Besides, what did he mean that he'd take care of me? I had no reason to trust anybody. At the same time, I was finding the work and the responsibilities hard going. I didn't know how long I could survive as a mother, a baby-minder and an over-stretched dogsbody working behind the bar in a late-night club. It wasn't the kind of life that anyone would choose to live – or anyone in their right mind, anyway.

"Don't worry, I'll find you somewhere to live," he told me. "I'll pay your rent. I'll look after you and your baby." I promised to think it over, though I honestly hadn't a clue what to make of a proposal that was both frightening and surprising. Looking back, I don't know whether I thought he'd fallen in love with me or was just being kind. Either way, I probably was less inhibited than most Irish girls at the time and there was something in me that was attracted to the possibility of an adventure. I kept turning the conversation over in my mind and wondering what did I have to lose? Not a lot, in the situation I was in.

The following week, I wasn't taken to the nightclub as normal. Somebody had told my boss that I had been seen in conversation with a strange man outside the house. It may seem bizarre from the perspective of the 1990s, but I was still young and she felt that that gave her the right to dictate what I could, and what I couldn't, do. It didn't matter that I'd already had a baby. She threatened to write to my parents and create all kinds of trouble for me.

When I look back, it seems strange that this threat would have assumed such an exaggerated sense of importance to me – but it did. The irony is that I was the only real mother this woman's own kids had known. I'd been her baby-sitter, housekeeper, bottle-washer, nanny, cook, cleaner, the whole caboodle, and all for no wages and even less appreciation. Now, under threat of being further exposed to my own mother, I gathered Philip and our few belongings and left this part of our lives behind. I knew that I was taking a risk – but I was driven by a desperate need to keep my independence intact and to experience the respect and warmth of another human being who cared for me.

My new American GI friend was called Jimmy Angel and he came from South Carolina. He fulfilled his promise and found us digs, which were nice if nothing special – but I now had the time and space to begin to get myself organised. And to begin to enjoy life again! After I moved in, I made friends with another girl who was also going out with an American. It was the beginning of a good phase in my life that I still remember fondly all these years later. Jimmy began taking Philip and me to the American base in which he was stationed, at Warrington in Cheshire. For the first time in my life, I was able to indulge in big, juicy T-bone steaks, nylon stockings, Hershey bars and all sorts of treats like barbecues that I'd never experienced before, and, in these still-rationed years, was otherwise not likely to experience for quite some while.

In time, I began a sexual relationship with Jimmy, putting Philip's father, who I believed was now living in Birmingham, behind me.

I still remained in contact with my sister Monica in Leeds and kept her informed about my developing friendship with Jimmy. One day, she invited us down and we all went to visit her in Jimmy's big car, with its green-tinted windows. Her house was situated on a hill, and sometime after we arrived, Philip, who was now almost three years old, went out to play with the other kids. I don't know how he did it but he managed somehow to get back into the car. He must have released the hand-brake, because the car took off down the hill with Philip in it. You can imagine the kind of fright I got when one of the neighbours raised the alarm. Luckily, neither the car nor Philip came to any harm, but he could have been seriously hurt. To say that he was now at the age when he demanded constant watching is to put it mildly.

Meanwhile, I was extremely happy in my relationship with Jimmy. He was a tall and very handsome man who took great pride in his appearance. From the time I had discovered him staring at me in the bar, I have to say that I was genuinely and thoroughly hooked on him.

I have never made any apology, and never will, for any of my relationships with black men. People should understand that many white men, as soon as they discovered I had a black baby, would have nothing to do with me anyway. It was awful to suffer rejection in this way – and so it was doubly uplifting to have a true friendship, where the colour of my skin and my child's skin were irrelevant.

At that time, I had very little confidence in my attractiveness to the opposite sex. Perhaps now, when I look back at photographs of myself in my early twenties, with my jet-black hair, I can see that I looked rather well, but I was not conscious of it then. On the contrary, when I used to look in the mirror before going out to a dance, despite being all dolled up, I never thought much of my appearance. I used to think my green eyes were like cat's eyes and I hated them.

I suppose part of the reason why I felt so lacking in self-confidence was that I had very little time to develop any awareness of my sexuality. I had become pregnant after having sex only a couple of times with the first man with whom I had a sexual liaison. I became a mother before I had the chance to enjoy anything like a full teenage life and I had to proceed through my life wary of getting pregnant a second time. But I never felt any resentment against men, neither then nor later. Jimmy had taken a shine to me, we had fallen in love – he had actually wanted to marry me at one point – and I was delighted to be rescued from the awful drudgery of the life I had been leading.

Of course, I had to deal with considerable inner trauma throughout that part of my life. The traditional teachings of the Catholic Church had been deeply ingrained in me since my earliest schooldays in Ireland and I had to accept that I was basically a sinner in the eyes of the church. An unmarried mother, with a black child, now living with a man I was not married to and who was not the father of my son: I was the kind of person that we'd all been taught to shun. Some inner part of me was probably deeply ashamed or riddled with guilt about the whole thing. It would take me a long time to rid myself of that horrible legacy, but eventually I did.

I have always believed that sex is beautiful, and once you have enjoyed it as a teenager you want it again. That is a perfectly natural response. Anyone who tries to suggest otherwise is plain daft. And there's nothing wrong with it either. Nothing.

That doesn't mean it's always going to be easy. While I endeavoured to cope with the practical pressures of my situation, I also had to deal with the various deep emotions I was experiencing and without anyone else to turn to or to share my feelings with, it was often very lonely.

Whether other people approve or not, I cannot alter what happened to me or the experiences I went through and I'm certainly not going to pretend that I'm sorry now for the sake of propriety. Of course, survival was the over-riding priority for me and my son, but I needed love and tenderness too and I got it, living very happily with Jimmy Angel for a couple of years. We were reasonably well off, with me drawing the dole while

Jimmy covered the cost of our lodgings and most other expenses. With his companionship, I was rediscovering that life could have some wonderful moments, and I reckon I was enjoying a reasonable share of them. No more than I deserved though, I can assure you!

Because I was drawing the dole, the welfare people one day demanded that I name Philip's natural father, and I had no alternative but to comply with their command. They in turn informed me that they were taking him to court to insist he pay me my due maintenance. Cecil, who was still sending me some money but with little regularity, then came to visit me in Manchester and told me he wanted Philip and me to live with him and that he wanted us to be married. I don't know whether or not he knew what he wanted at all – or the level of responsibility involved in bringing up a child. Either way, that prospect no longer had any appeal for me, assuming it ever had, because I was now extremely content with Jimmy and we were in love with each other, so when I refused his proposal, Cecil was so incensed that he threatened to take Philip away from me.

When the case came to court, I was terrified. The cold, grey court-house, and the snooty, stern-faced barristers who swaggered and strutted through the long corridors with their wigs and gowns, did little to reassure me. In the event, Cecil did not appear in person but instead wrote a letter to the magistrate in effect saying, "I am Cecil Parris. I do not deny the parentage of the said child and whatever you decide that I should pay towards his maintenance I will willingly do so."

Cecil's generous and frank admission not only surprised me after his threat to take Philip, but his attitude was in sharp contrast to the other cases I observed while attending the court, where the usual approach was for the man to deny fatherhood so that blood-tests were often required. When Cecil's letter was read out, I was absolutely thrilled because it put the whole issue of Philip's parentage forever completely beyond a shadow of doubt. Here was an honest man courageously accepting, without any prevarication, that he was the natural father of my son. A spiteful man could have denied his responsibility and thereby caused me endless grief, but that was not Cecil's nature and it made me eternally grateful to him for his honesty.

Obviously, the kind of situation I found myself in reflects much of the bias against women that is too common in our society, even today. A man can have sex with a woman, and if she gets pregnant she is literally left holding the baby while the man can deny all knowledge and evade all responsibility. But Cecil behaved very honourably, despite the fact that it might not have been easy for him, particularly since I had refused his offer of marriage. I know I loved him at one point, but after discovering that he was two-timing me, I was not convinced that I wanted to spend the rest of my life with him.

My sister Monica made it abundantly clear to me how she felt about him. She would have been bitterly opposed to him when she realised how he had been behaving with other women after he knew I had borne his child. She told me quite bluntly "If you marry him, I'll swing for you." And she meant it.

Although I was tremendously relieved at the outcome of the court case, there were further difficulties ahead. My happy life with Jimmy Angel was not destined to last for very much longer. While America is still troubled by racism today, the situation at that time was far worse. Blacks in certain states were forced to sit in segregated sections of restaurants, cinemas and buses, and this bigoted, separatist outlook was reflected in the attitudes of large portions of the ordinary American public. There were many of Jimmy's fellow Americans at the base in Warrington who objected to his close association with a white woman. As time passed, the antagonism towards him increased and he was eventually transferred to another base overseas, apparently for his own safety. Soon he was gone almost completely from my life except for the letters we regularly exchanged.

Naturally, and inevitably I suppose, we gradually lost touch and, after I became reconciled to the permanence of his departure, I hoped that he might find his way back to his old routine in South Carolina and, for all I know, maybe he married his childhood sweetheart. But Philip took his absence very badly.

At approximately the same time, Philip was beginning to be the direct recipient of the same kind of disgusting racial taunts that had previously been hurled at me. One instance occurred in the Chorlton area of Manchester during a period when we were living with a family called Nimro. There was a friendly, neighbourly woman who often shared with us some of the tasty bread she used to bake in her house.

One day, I sent Philip to collect some from her and, when some considerable time had elapsed with no sign of him returning, I anxiously set off in search of him.

Not far along the road, I came upon two kids playing near the road, with another up a tree throwing chestnuts down to them. Before I could ask them if they had seen my Philip, I realised that the boy up the tree was Philip. When I chastised the boys for encouraging such a small boy to climb a tree, they told me that he was well able to climb trees because he was a monkey! I know the children meant no harm, but that example shows what dreadful prejudices were planted in the minds of innocent white kids concerning members of other races.

Sadly, even in the so-called liberal 1990s, there are too many similar instances where the same blind ignorance forms an integral part of the world in which innocent children grow up. One wonders if such bigotry will always be with us? But with Jimmy Angel only recently having departed from his life, Philip was being forced to begin learning how to face such ignorance – and he had not yet even started attending school.

A TALE OF TWO CITIES

We stayed on in Manchester after Jimmy's departure and it was not long before my parents came over to visit my sister Monica in Leeds. Monica then suggested that they should travel down to Manchester to meet Philip, who was three years old by then, for the first time.

It was bound to be a difficult occasion for everyone involved and for some time beforehand I had been preparing Philip by repeatedly telling him, "You're going to meet your grandma and your grandad." For days the poor kid had been repeating the words 'grandma' and 'grandad' over and over.

Inevitably, by the time we got to Victoria Railway Station, Philip was very excited by all the fuss. And it got worse. There was no sign of my parents but as we waited, I noticed a commotion centred around a group of about ten men passing through the station. The object of everyone's attention was a well-known Red Indian wrestler called Billy Two-Rivers, who as it happens lived very close to my flat and who later became a national celebrity on British television because of his spectacular Red Indian wrestling style.

Just then, I spotted my mother approaching us with tears in her eyes. But before she got to us, Billy rushed over, lifted me up and swung me around, right there in front of her. She, of course, did not know that, being neighbours, we knew each other rather well and so she was astonished at what was going on in public, between her daughter and a huge, burly man with a very weird Mohican hair-style (of exactly the kind which, oddly enough, was to become very popular with so many young people about two decades later – I guess Billy was before his time!). My father, was so taken aback that he could only burst out, "Sacred Heart of Jaysus!" – an exclamation that could be heard all over the station. As we found out later, he thought Billy Two-Rivers was Philip's dad! I will never forget the expression on my father's face as long as I live, with the whole station, including little Philip, looking on in amazement at this extraordinary spectacle. What a way for my parents to meet my son for the first time!

After an initial tentativeness, Mam and Dad discovered that they really liked Philip, who was an extremely lovable kid and, from that point, they enjoyed a very close relationship with him for as long as they both lived. To help cement the new relationship, I invited them for a little holiday to where we were now living, in Didsbury, and made as much of a fuss of them as I could because I knew only too well how tough all this was for them. I remember having a lovely time, but of course it couldn't last and they returned to Dublin. At least now, however, I felt reassured of the love of my parents – not just for me, but for Philip also. That was very important because I was gradually finding it harder and harder to cope on my own.

At this distance, it seems virtually impossible to convey the difficulty faced by a young unmarried mother in the early 1950s, trying to hold on to her child in the kind of circumstances I found myself in, striving to dress, feed and clothe him while holding down demanding jobs – and at the same time having to do whatever you could to protect yourself in a very vulnerable and lonely predicament. Even a trip to the local shop can become a big ordeal in such situations and for me that's how it had begun to feel.

There were times when I had no job and food was a major problem. Through one bad patch, I remember cooking a pan of porridge over an open coal fire for myself and Philip and putting some of it aside for the next morning's breakfast. That was all the food we had. Another time, my resources had sunk to the point where I was reduced to asking the butcher for some bones which I pretended were for a dog. Later, I added one carrot, one onion and a couple of small potatoes to those bones to make us a stew.

To add to the obvious problems of racism, loneliness and poverty, I also had to endure occasional public indignities which I can only put down to the fact that Philip was black. It came to a head one day when I was queueing for a bus, hungry and bitterly cold, with Philip in his buggy. When the bus pulled up at the stop, I expected the conductor to offer the customary courtesy of helping me on with the buggy. But on this occasion, to my great distress, he didn't lift a finger. Instead of helping me, he maliciously rang the bell for the bus to move on without us. This was the last straw for me, and I collapsed on the street. A woman went for assistance to a nearby chemist and they brought me a glass of ice-cold water with some peppermint which was hardly much help in the state I was in.

I think that was the straw that broke the camel's back. I had been under pressure for a long time but had kept going, unaware of how close I was to complete and total physical exhaustion. That incident finally brought it home to me that it was no longer feasible for me to care for Philip adequately on my own. I suppose it became obvious to me that I was in serious danger of permanently damaging my own health, and possibly even Philip's. I certainly had reached the point where I simply could not bear any more hardship.

I sometimes wonder might I have done things differently – and how would our lives have turned out if I had? In the face of overwhelming difficulties, I had struggled to avoid becoming too depressed and I certainly never sank so low, in spite of the pressures, as to contemplate anything as drastic as suicide. Nor did I pray very often, probably because I had become so utterly disillusioned by this so-called Christian society and the hateful way it had treated me and my innocent baby. But I was desperately in need of help and there didn't seem to be a great deal of it about in Manchester at the time.

Things might have been different if all this had happened in the 1960s because of the developments which took place in the Welfare State and in particular in the level of support for unmarried mothers – but in the 1950s that support just wasn't available. Against that background, the avenues of escape for us from the predicament we faced were few and far between. Cecil and I were by now living totally separate lives. He was not sending me the maintenance money which the court had ordered him to, but I had no stomach for the prospect of having to pursue him for it. And, besides, I had neither the inclination nor the resources to embark on a legal battle – at least partly because I realised that if you looked at it from *his* perspective, I had selfishly taken his child away from him.

Equally, there was no point in me harbouring plans to move back to Dublin with Philip because this was still the dour, depressed 50s and the chronic jobs situation in Ireland had not improved. People were emigrating in their droves, so how could I expect to get a job?

Marriage was not an option either, given my circumstances at that time. In those narrow-minded days, it was tough even for women who had given birth to illegitimate white babies to form new relationships. As a result, back-street abortions were common and many unfortunate women in similar positions to me had no alternative but to go down that road. I have met several of them since and they are amazed that I stubbornly insisted on continuing my pregnancy, notwithstanding that I had made that crude attempt at abortion myself.

I have never understood where my stubbornness came from, since my sisters were all rather quiet, inoffensive and easy-going. Perhaps it developed in me as a direct response to the pressures which were assailing me on all fronts. Or maybe it's just the way that I was born, because even today I will not tolerate anybody talking down to me.

There are some people who meet me and who probably leave with the impression that I am a hard woman, while perhaps others might think more kindly of me. But I do know that I was faced with hard decisions along the way and that I had to make them on my own. So, after much heart-searching and agonised deliberation, I decided that the only sensible course of action was for me to ask Mum to take Philip into her house in Dublin while I would stay in England. It was hard to ask, I don't mind saying, because I had to swallow my pride to do so. It was even harder because the prospect of being separated from Philip was an appalling one. But I knew that I would be relieved too of a burden of responsibility that I was finding increasingly difficult to bear. It could, I know, seem like a very selfish option to have chosen, but I can say this much for certain – it didn't feel like that at the time.

About a year after the emotional reunion with my parents and their first meeting with Philip in Manchester, I wrote to Mum and asked her to consider taking Philip to live with her in Dublin.

In my head, I knew that sending Philip to Dublin was the right thing to do. But, in my heart, I was torn apart with sorrow at the very idea. When Mum kindly agreed, however, I decided to go through with it, for my own sake as much as for Philip's. Mum fully understood that I needed the break, otherwise I would never be free to build a real life for myself.

I promised to send her as much money as I could spare, and I intended to look out for clothes for Philip since I would probably pick up better bargains in Manchester than my mother could afford to buy in Dublin. That kind of thinking might seem crazy now but it's the way your mind works in a situation like that. You focus on the inconsequential details a lot of the time, in an effort to shut out the harsh realities.

I will never forget the morning when I had to leave four-year-old Philip behind in Dublin, while I returned alone to Manchester. As I packed my bag for the journey, my fingers were literally trembling with anguish and distress. I couldn't speak properly. The muscles around my throat had tightened, and I could barely look at Philip without wanting to cry. After everything we had been through together I could only hope that he wouldn't experience it as a betrayal, and that he would settle down and be happy in my absence. With all the strength I could muster, I fixed a smile firmly on my face and cuddled Philip for all my life was worth, whispering to him that it wouldn't be long before we would be together again. At the same time I knew that I was lucky that I had a loving mother and father to turn to. So many young women in circumstances similar to my own don't.

I returned to Manchester and soon afterwards, I picked up three part-time jobs, including one on a stall in an open market and another as a barmaid. Although my standard of living and my health had both improved somewhat now that I did not have a small child to look after, life was still far from rosy. My child, for whom I had sacrificed so much to hold on to, was now in another country. Living on my own again since Jimmy Angel's overseas posting, there was very little in the way of joy in my life. It was an austere time generally. All my clothes were purchased from second-hand stores or from market stalls. I was constantly on the look-out for bargains and did a lot of my shopping at Woolworths, where you could purchase popular items like Evening In Paris perfume for two shillings and sixpence. In fact, I still have one of those distinctive blue bottles which I kept as a memento. It also serves as a constant reminder of a memorable occasion on a train journey with Philip when he was only about three years old. Out of the blue, he said to me, "Ma, you smell lovely," and when I explained to him about perfume he said, "When I grow up I'm going to buy you lots and lots of perfume and a big, big house." He did buy me the house and, right from the time he first started travelling, he never came home without a bottle of perfume for me.

It goes without saying that there was real consolation in the knowledge that Philip was now living in a secure, loving household with a standard of life which, though relatively poor by modern standards, was a lot better than anything I could have provided for him at the time. He now had regular food, proper nourishing meals and a clean, warm bed among people who cared for him and loved him. Yet my heart still ached to have him with me. I derived some pleasure from writing regular letters to my mother and I'd enclose as much money as I could afford, but the heavy workload meant I had no time to build friendships with either sex.

Not that the situation was without its difficulties for my family in Dublin. When Philip first moved in with them, the social pressures were so intense that the family conspired to pretend to their neighbours that Philip was the son of a friend of mine or that his mother had died. Indeed, they'd have spun any yarn they thought people would swallow to avoid telling the truth. And you couldn't blame them. The level of shame and embarrassment which surrounded the idea of a child being born to an unmarried mother in Ireland at the time was frightening. And so numerous estates all over Dublin had their mystery children – kids who appeared out of nowhere at the age of three or four or five and no-one quite knew for sure were they adopted, were they family – or were they just staying for a while . . .

In retrospect, it has to be admitted that it was extremely courageous of my Mam to take Philip in. There was no way his presence in the house wasn't going to become a source of unpleasant gossip, given the social and religious climate of the time, and especially given that he was a little black boy. To say that he'd stand out in Dublin in 1954 is to put it mildly! Besides, she already had her hands sufficiently full with my father Frank, my ten-year-old sister Irene and my younger brothers Tim who was seven, and Peter who was only a year older than Philip.

For her courage and limitless generosity, I have been always deeply grateful to Mam. When she was herself coming to the end of her life, I was able to return the favour, albeit in a very small way by ensuring that she would not have to enter a home and I treasure the memory of holding her in my arms when she died.

Living on my own, I no longer had to endure the unpleasant innuendo or the outright offensive remarks that I had often been subjected to while Philip was with me, except on those occasions when I visited Dublin, about five times each year. Back home, I found myself defiantly fighting my ingrained Irish tendency towards being ashamed of my circumstances. There was a constant process of awakening taking place within me, as I constantly questioned the conventional attitudes my upbringing had instilled in me and virtually every other young woman of my generation.

Illegitimate offspring – an offensive term in itself, as if the birth of any human being could actually be deemed illegitimate – are often referred to as 'love children', but in my time they were considered 'sin children'. You were expected to hang your head in shame if you gave birth out of wedlock. It was not until I reached my thirties that I finally shook off the last residues of that shame. I have always resented the fact that it has traditionally been the pregnant woman who has been despised. How many others in my time were enjoying sexual relationships and were lucky enough to avoid becoming pregnant? And why was there no shame attached to the men in any of these situations? And what is wrong, anyway, with love freely given and freely shared? And if a child results, is it not the most important thing that he or she, in turn, is loved?

It was that sense of shame, unjustly imposed by an intolerant society, which forced my family to keep up one pretence or another about Philip for several years, but I believe that most of the neighbours saw through it and knew he was mine. For my mother's sake, and her sake alone, I played along with her stories, but before those who dared to look me in the eye and defy me to tell the truth, I would openly behave as if, yes, he was indeed my son and the more often I visited Crumlin, the more rebellious I became in the face of the offensive taunts I would be subjected to by some of the more vicious and narrow-minded neighbours.

Like many other working class areas of Dublin, Crumlin was a tough place to grow up in. Located on the south west of the city, there's nothing intrinsically attractive or pretty about it. Row upon row of faceless, terraced houses to some degree obscured the depths of poverty which often existed side by side with the relative prosperity of others. It was easy to lose yourself in the anonymity of the estates, which ran like rabbit warrens throughout the area. While violence and crime were not uncommon, it was, for the most part in those days, a seemingly friendly place with a real sense of community spirit. Behind closed doors, however, all manner of prejudices were nurtured, and gossip, both malicious and harmless, was as much a part of the daily diet as potatoes, cabbage and – for those who could afford them – pork chops.

One particular Crumlin neighbour would regularly, and very pointedly, remark to me, while looking at Philip, "Isn't he just like you when you were a child?" I suppose I should have taken it as a compliment but I don't think it was intended that way. When he was about seven, the local shopkeeper very skittishly passed a similar remark and I couldn't restrain myself from shouting back at him, "I know, sure isn't he mine?".

Small incidents linger on in the mind, which suggest that there was a horrible kind of stress in maintaining the pretence. On another occasion when we were out shopping, Philip had smeared chocolate all over his face. I must have been reaching breaking point with the way we were being treated, because when a woman went to wipe his face, I said, "Oh look, the colour comes off." I said it with real venom and bitterness, and I can still remember the anger I felt welling up inside me.

It'd be easy to conclude that I was being paranoid, but there was a dreadful, parochial small-mindedness about. While travelling on the ferry between Holyhead and Ireland, I once overheard a group of people gossiping about "a girl over on Kildare Road in Crumlin who had given birth to a black baby." They agreed how shocking it all was. As it happened, I was acquainted with the girl under discussion. Cathleen was her name and, when I arrived in Dublin again, I called to her house to show her that she was not the only one in that particular predicament, and to offer her some advice based on my own experience.

Of course, not all Irish people were so petty and so prim – there were many good-natured individuals who would compliment me on my beautiful child and some who would stare admiringly at his lovely hair and ask me for a curl.

Meantime, while I was away in Manchester, my mother coped admirably. She had given birth to my younger brother, Peter, at the grand old age of 51. As he was only one year older than Philip, she raised the two of them together as if they were brothers. Indeed she had nine children in total, so Philip, growing up with his uncles Peter and Tim for company, was not the enormous extra burden for her that some people might imagine. That was one of the good things about the kind of large families so many people in Ireland had at the time – to an extent the kids took care of one another and even though it was hard for mothers in particular, adding another one to the flock wasn't the major decision it sometimes seems like nowadays.

· The passage of time had helped my mother recover from the shock of Philip's birth and his colour. My father Frank, meanwhile, like many Dublin working-class men of that era, dutifully went to and from work each day and popped out for his pint in the local at night. They were happy together and I suppose the pretence about Philip's origins probably helped him more than anybody else in that respect. Much as he loved Philip, I don't think he'd have been comfortable if he'd had to explain the circumstances to his friends. Sadly, he died of a heart-attack in May 1964 and Philip, who was only fourteen at the time, was heartbroken. Because of his sudden death, his grandfather missed out on all of Philip's later successes, which he would have thoroughly enjoyed, as he was the first to spot the showman in the young Philip.

On my trips home, I would treat Philip, his uncle Peter and my nephew, Ronnie, to whatever was appropriate at the time, whether to a pantomime, a visit to Santa or to the cinema. Alternatively, I might simply take them shopping in the centre of Dublin, which was considered a real treat for children then, although few of today's worldly-wise kids would be so impressed! We would have great fun together, but it was heartbreaking having to leave Philip behind each time I returned to Manchester.

Visits home also afforded me the opportunity to go dancing and to contact some of my Dublin friends. Mostly these were good times – Philip, I knew, was safe and I didn't have to worry about the prospect of having to get up for work the next day – but there were incidents also which underlined the fact that my experiences marked me down as an outsider. I remember cycling to the house of Geraldine, a pal of mine who was now married, and while I was there her husband Harry arrived in. It did not take me long to spot that he was very much the worse for drink. When the time came for me to leave, Harry was persuaded to show me a short-cut back to Mam's house.

We were both on bikes, but after we had cycled only part of the way he cut across me and then tried to push me up against a wall, where he drunkenly attempted to have sexual intercourse with me. Horrified by his behaviour, I pushed him away, but that made him even more furious, and he shouted at me, "You let the niggers have you but one of your own kind is not good enough for you." Thankfully he didn't become violent as he might have, but I was so appalled and frightened that I could never bring myself to meet Geraldine again. In a way, I regret that I could not pluck up the courage to tell her the reason why – I probably should have, since it was not her who had tried to rape me, but then, who knows how she would have responded or what the effect on their relationship might have been?

Unfortunately, that sort of reaction from men was not uncommon. On the rare occasions when I had time to go out for a date, I could see the adverse response as soon as I admitted that I had had an illegitimate child. For some of them, inevitably, my child's colour was the central problem. Also, the fact that I told them about Philip upfront often seemed to be taken as an indication that I must be a sex-starved nymphomaniac only too keen to jump into bed with any man who offered himself. It was a constant dilemma that seemed to rear its head almost as soon as I thought any man might be taking a genuine fancy to me. I had the awful choice of telling the truth early on, or allowing the relationship to develop and then probably having it ruined anyway, as soon as the truth was revealed.

Sadly, that kind of overt racism is still to be encountered to this day, although I like to think it is not quite as prevalent as it was in my time. Back then, I could not help worrying how Philip, growing up in a tough, no-holds-barred area of Dublin, was going to cope with this problem. I knew it inevitably would catch up with him, and my family's protection would not shield him forever.

"Uncle Peter
was writing
a book/
and his Mama
was starting
to cook."

– from 'Saga Of The Ageing Orphan' by Philip Lynott

There was no doubt that Philip was happy growing up in Crumlin. When he was disobedient, he was disciplined by my parents like any other child, but they got on extremely well and he liked being part of a big family. Inevitably, he suffered racial prejudice in school. Yet, despite the inevitable difficulties caused by his colour – which, in fairness, to some children was merely an innocent source of novelty – he was popular in the neighbourhood. As soon as he learned to write, his letters to me were an added comfort. He had a natural way with words and he shared many of his highs and lows with me through his correspondence.

Somebody who knew more about these things than I did might just have spotted the germ of a poetic talent in those letters.

In the meantime, Philip had also begun to exhibit the signs of a confident showman. He used to clown around a lot, putting lampshades on his head, pulling funny faces and general play-acting. My father, who used to encourage him, often said that he reminded him of Sammy Davis Jnr, who was also black, and a hell of an entertainer.

One thing was certain, Philip was never shy, although I cannot imagine that he got that confidence from me. I had been reared through the war years and, like most Irish working-class people, we never thought we had anything going for us. Indeed, personal confidence only grew in me in later life.

Apart from his developing gregariousness and his entertaining tomfoolery, there were other early signs that music would become his life – though I'd never have dreamt it at the time. I remember that I caught him one day with a bunch of his pals in the house in Crumlin, giggling and whispering. After much probing, he admitted he was going to a concert in a small wooden hall near Mount Argus, not far from where he lived. What he didn't tell me – though one of his pals did secretly – was that he was going to sing at the concert.

One of my sisters and I decided to attend, unknown to Philip, and I hid behind a tall priest in the audience to prevent him from seeing me. He came on stage with his band as if he had been born to it, wearing a single glove and singing a pop song of the day. That was the first time I saw him performing on stage and I was genuinely amazed at his self-assurance. I won't claim that I spotted straightaway that he was a star in the making – but I was impressed.

As he grew older, he had become greatly taken with his uncle Tim's record collection and they often went shopping together for the latest releases. Philip would avidly listen to whatever they bought – Tim was a fan of black American soul music, of British blues-rock bands like John Mayall's Bluesbreakers and Cream and even of American west coast artists like The Mamas And Papas – and Philip was influenced by all of these different types of music. Indeed, Tim may have later regretted fostering this love of music because when Philip moved to London, he took much of Tim's prized collection with him!

Apart from Tim's record collection, Philip's musical interests would also have been stimulated by his uncle Peter, who played guitar and sang in a band called The Sundowners. When Peter, (who eventually made it into rock music history by being mentioned in Philip's song-poem, 'Saga

Of The Ageing Orphan', recorded for Thin Lizzy's first album) turned down an invitation to join a local band, Philip jumped at the offer in his stead.

However, the first real indication I had that his musical ambitions might be serious and long-term came when I saw him singing in a band called The Black Eagles who, unknown to me, had become really popular all over Dublin. They played at venues like The Five Club, The Flamingo, and Club A Go-Go, as well as gigging outside the city, and by all accounts, Philip – who was just fifteen at the time – was beginning to revel in the modest level of local celebrity he had earned.

Back in Manchester, one of my regular jobs during 1966 was as a cashier for a Mr. Harold Marsden, who ran an open market trading business on Saturdays. Every Saturday, he would treat his son Peter and myself to a beautiful meal after we had finished our work duties for the day. During one of those dinners in a nearby nightclub, a Mr. Kent who owned The Clifton Grange Hotel, in Whalley Range in Manchester, confided to Harold that he would have to sell up because he was becoming increasingly concerned about the way it was being managed. I have no idea what inspired him but Harold interjected, saying, "Why not let Philomena run it for you?" I knew nothing about hotels but after talking it over with my new male companion Dennis Keeley, I figured it'd be worth looking at the set-up at least. The Clifton Grange Hotel, we discovered, was a detached old Victorian house on the corner of Manchester's Wellington Road. The house had been converted for use as digs, specialising in a showbusiness clientele. It had a somewhat rundown appearance, but inside it had a character and charm all its own – never mind the characters who stayed there!

When we sat down to discuss things, Mr. Kent threw me a little off-balance by inquiring whether I had any money to invest as a partner. When I told him that I didn't have those kind of resources, he opted to appoint me as manager of the business. Needless to say, I was thrilled. It was a lucky break and, what's more, he had no objection to Dennis working with me, so that we could develop the business and earn a living while also consolidating our relationship. It was such a unique opportunity that we both determined to work our fingers to the bone and to do whatever would be necessary to make the business work. We gave it everything, so that when the owner, who was himself a qualified accountant, reviewed the situation after a few months, he was so impressed by my scrupulously accurate bookwork that he bought me an enormous box of chocolates. Then he took me to his solicitor and made me joint owner of the business on the spot. Can you imagine how astonished I was, after all I had been through since Philip's birth?

BIRTH OF THE ROCKER

On Thin Lizzy's debut album, released in 1971, there is a song called 'Clifton Grange Hotel', inspired by the hotel and its unique atmosphere, lifestyle and clientele. And boy, was it unique. Graham Cohen started working for me at the hotel shortly after I began to act as manager. He was aged eighteen when we first met and he is still a close friend and colleague. Percy Gibbons, another dear friend of mine to this day, was already firmly ensconced there with his band, as were a troupe of Maoris from New Zealand, a young couple called Shirley and Johnny, a whole menagerie of cabaret singers, dancers, magicians, strippers, ventriloquists, comedians and many more colourful characters – among them a drag artist who always insisted on using the ladies' toilet!

The hotel was situated in the Whalley Range area of Manchester and I grew very fond of the people who lived around us because they were essentially down to earth, ordinary folks like ourselves, with no pretensions. The bar was a glorious hotchpotch, a mix of antique decor and all kind of knick-knacks, with dolls and flowers and other stuff hanging from the beams that crossed the low ceiling. On the walls, we displayed mock-autographed photographs of film stars like Gregory Peck and Sammy Davis Jnr. To be honest, I loved the place and enjoyed running the business so much that after just 18 months working there, I took my courage in my hands, arranged a bank loan and bought the Clifton Grange for the price Mr Kent had originally paid for it himself. That's how Philomena Lynott from Crumlin, Dublin became the proud owner of a hotel in Manchester, virtually overnight!

No doubt about it, the tide was finally turning in my favour, after years of poverty, abuse and dejection. By the time I had finalised the purchase of the hotel, I was also enjoying a deeply loving and stable relationship with Dennis Keeley, whom I'd first met in Didsbury in Manchester when Philip was about thirteen or fourteen, and who would become my life-long companion.

Of all the white men I have had friendships with, Dennis is the only one who has never exhibited any jealousy of Philip. In fact they struck up a rapport right from the first time they met. Dennis and I had been happily living together for quite some time when I announced that my son, whom Dennis knew was black, was coming over from Ireland to meet him. I explained to Dennis that it would be improper for us to sleep together while my innocent teenage son was in the house and a separate room was arranged for the two males. Of course, Philip wasn't nearly as innocent as I imagined.

Dennis can still recall waking up during the night and seeing Philip sitting up in his bed very sheepishly, but when they looked at each other in the morning they both burst out laughing – conscious I suppose, of the absurdity of the situation. Philip later admitted he knew only too well that we were sleeping together, and could not understand why I had chosen to pretend otherwise. I explained that it was a question of respect, though what I actually *meant* by that, I'm not too sure. He and Dennis were later to become really close buddies and they would regularly go shopping together, despite Philip's irritating habit of spending ages chatting up all the girls working in the shops!

It was around the same time that, during a visit to Dublin, I noticed that Philip's teeth had badly deteriorated. I flew him over to Manchester for three successive weekends to a great dentist I knew called Hans Kurer, on whose wall hung a motto, "Pain Is Forbidden In This Room." Young Philip told him he was the greatest dentist in the whole world, and he was not far wrong, as Doctor Kurer was later honoured with an O.B.E. by Queen Elizabeth ll.

Overall, however, Philip was a very healthy, wiry teenager, who kept himself fit playing football. The first time he was in hospital was in 1969. Philip was in Skid Row at the time, and probably as a result of the rigours of singing against a very loud and noisy backing band, his tonsils had swollen to a phenomenal size. Again, I flew him over to Manchester, to a private hospital called St. Joseph's, where they removed the tonsils. Brush Shiels, who was the leader of Skid Row, had apparently been troubled by the deteriorating quality of Philip's voice. While Philip was undergoing his operation, the band did some gigs without him and then decided to continue without him permanently. Or, to put it more bluntly, he was sacked. As you can imagine, that decision hit him pretty hard, but he had enough confidence in his own ability not to let it get him down, and he remained friends with Brush down the years.

Because Philip and I were apart most of the time, we made the most of our occasional get-togethers, no matter what the circumstances. In some respects, our relationship was more like brother and sister than mother and son. We behaved as if we were best friends, sharing all our joys and at least some of our heartaches. Philip often came over to us in Manchester with my own mother, who was, not surprisingly, overwhelmed by the weird and wonderful characters she would bump into in various parts of The Biz or The Showbiz, which were colloquial names for the Clifton Grange Hotel in Manchester. In virtually every respect, it was a world which was completely removed from her conventional upbringing in conservative, guilt-ridden Ireland, but she liked it all the same.

During one visit, we took Philip and my brother Peter to a popular cabaret club in Manchester and secretly arranged for the compere to introduce Philip as the night's special guest performer. Despite Philip's obvious surprise, not to mention embarrassment, he did a pretty impressive version of 'I Left My Heart In San Francisco' in a style that could not have offered a greater contrast to his subsequent international tough-guy image as 'The Rocker'.

My immediate circle of Manchester friends included Percy Gibbons, whom I've already mentioned – he was a member of a highly successful three-piece all-black Canadian cabaret act called The Other Brothers. He was already entrenched in his favourite psychedelically-decorated attic room at the Clifton Grange Hotel, long before Dennis and I first moved there. When Percy's band went on the road, he insisted his room had to be either closed up or only let to people he approved of – for example Philip, with whom he had developed a close relationship based on their mutual obsession with music.

Predictably, Philip was in awe of Percy, who had been living in Manchester since 1964, and was really a striking character. While it has to be acknowledged that Brush Shiels in Dublin played a major role in Philip's early development as a musician, I have a feeling that Percy was an equally significant influence, not merely in the artistic sense but because he also made a terrific impression on Philip's personality and behaviour as well. Philip practised incessantly on Percy's guitar and they would discuss music, politics, racism and show-business non-stop at every available opportunity.

Whenever they got the opportunity, the two of them would sing, play guitars and bongos and write songs together in Percy's room. Some of the ideas that later turned up in Thin Lizzy songs had their origin in those jam sessions and I believe Philip was heavily inspired by the fact that a black band like The Other Brothers could get on in spite of the fact that they were black. For his part, Percy has also admitted to me that he, in turn, learned a lot from Philip's determination and commitment. When he later saw Thin Lizzy in full flight, it encouraged his own band to update what he came to acknowledge was a somewhat dated style.

In the song, 'Clifton Grange Hotel', Philip refers, perhaps with some degree of poetic license, to the place as "*a refuge of mercy*" but there's no doubt that he loved coming over. He referred to "*Old Lou the Jew who will take your bags from you*" – Lou was a real character, and a nice man with whom Philip got on very well – while Percy gets an oblique mention when Philip sings about "another brother." I think I even get a namecheck myself!

Rock 'n' roll trivia fans may be interested to know that I had earlier, if a little misguidedly, attempted to persuade Percy to take Philip into his band which, in the wake of the Beatles' revolution, had been given the more psychedelic name of Garden Odyssey. Percy may have recognised that Philip's long-term musical ambitions lay in other directions and in a different musical style. Either way, that particular musical marriage was never consummated.

Such were the close ties of friendship that had grown up in and around the hotel that, when Christmas came, Philip, Percy, Roy and Dennis would all compete with great gusto to see who could buy me the best present, which one year included a mynah bird! I was a lucky woman, surrounded by such good, close friends in such a wonderful, family atmosphere. I don't recall ever hearing harsh words between any of them. Even I, his mother, only had one serious row with Philip in my life. That occurred years later when I discovered he had given away, to a roadie, a very expensive suitcase I had bought him, a green leather Antler model with his initials specially engraved on it. Perhaps the nature of that single disagreement best explains the closeness of the relationship we enjoyed.

"It's three o'clock in the morning
And I'm on the streets again
I disobeyed another warning
I should have been in by ten"
– from 'Dancing In The Moonlight' by Philip Lynott

My brother Timothy was getting married during 1967 and Dennis, Percy and another musician by the name of Roy Ellis, and I, all came over to Dublin for the wedding in Malahide, a picturesque seaside suburb to the north of Dublin not too far from where I live now. Philip was about 17 at the time and he pleaded not to be forced into singing at the wedding because he had a gig in a Dublin night-club that same night. After the wedding, all four of us went along to the club, which I remember was in a cellar. I can recall relaxing nonchalantly against a pillar until my reverie was interrupted by a large group of girls screaming. I looked up and realised that they were screaming for Philip who had just come on stage. It was only my second time to see him performing and I was stunned by how good he and his band were. Percy, who really knows his music, turned to me and said in amazement: "Isn't Philip brilliant!" I said, "Percy, you took the words right out of my mouth, but because you might think I'm biased, I didn't want to say anything." I was convinced then that Philip had something special. For me, it was a night to remember.

Within a month or two, Mam rang me in Manchester to ask me to come to Dublin again because Philip was proving a bit of a handful. She was convinced he was heading for trouble with the police, hanging around with what she felt was a rough lot of young lads and staying out until three or four in the morning. The final straw, it seemed, had come when he arrived home having lost one of his expensive new shoes.

Most teenagers go through a rebellious phase and Philip was probably no different, but even his uncle Peter – who was only a year older than my boy – was becoming increasingly disenchanted with Philip's behaviour whenever they went to a club together. His grandfather having passed away, there may have been an absence of an authority figure who could control Philip's wilder impulses and so poor Tim was cast in that role. On one occasion he became so frustrated with Philip that he locked him out of the house when he did not arrive home by the appointed hour one night. Afterwards, he gave Philip a serious ticking off, but to no avail, apparently.

It's curious how these things work. This was a really traumatic period for everyone else in the family. They were worried, probably unnecessarily, about Philip. But for him it was to become the inspiration for one of Thin Lizzy's best and most successful hit songs, 'Dancing In The

Moonlight', with its references to the narrator being out on the street until three o'clock in the morning, disobeying warnings and being kept indoors as a punishment.

However much he was enjoying being the rebel, I felt that the problem needed to be tackled urgently and, being a little more flush with funds because of the success of Clifton Grange, I flew over to Dublin immediately. Of course, when I challenged him about the lost shoe, I got all the predictable excuses a mother usually gets from a son in situations like this. His story was that the band had been down the country doing a gig and the manager had arranged for them to sleep in tents, presumably to save money on hotel bills. They were a bunch of lads enjoying a teenage adventure together and they behaved accordingly. During a bout of typical, boyish play-acting one of his shoes went missing, never to be found. And then he told me that he had his own grievances – he was genuinely upset because his grandmother thought his friends looked like gypsies on account of their style of dress, and she would not allow any of them into her house. And it's fair to say that a lot of parents and teenagers were experiencing similar conflicts at the time.

One of those who was being excluded from the Lynott household was Brian Downey, who later turned out to be a loyal friend to both Philip and to myself and who stuck by Philip throughout all the highs and lows of Thin Lizzy's career. Philip had first met Brian, who was a little younger than him, when they attended the same school, the Christian Brothers school in Crumlin. (Incidentally, while attending that particular school, Philip had been insensitively given the chore of collecting money from the schoolboys for what was called "the Black Babies", but in reality was for the Catholic Missionaries in Africa.) I must admit that I had some sympathy for Philip. At the same time, my mother was entitled to run her house however she saw fit, and she was certainly entitled to have her wishes respected by Philip, to whom she'd given so much.

Philip himself was intelligent enough to understand fully why his Gran was upset and how, as long as he was living under the same roof as her,

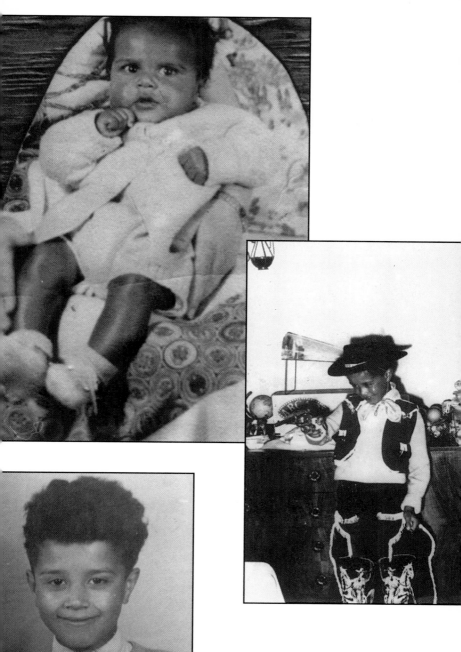

EARLY DAYS *(Clockwise from top)*:
Philip aged three months; enacting
The Cowboy Song on his fifth birthday; and in a school photograph, aged
six.

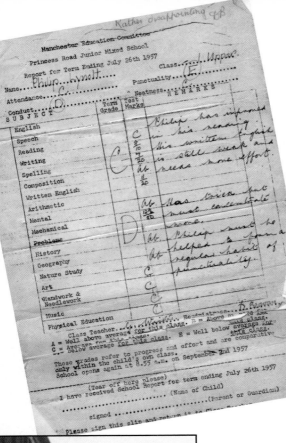

Rather disappointing &B

Manchester Education Committee
Princess Road Junior Mixed School
Report for Term Ending July 26th 1957

Name...Philip...Lynott....   Class....1..Upper.
Attendance....O   Punctuality....E....
Conduct....O   Neatness....

SUBJECT	Term Grade	Test Marks	REMARKS
English			Philip has improved
Speech	C	8/10	in his reading
Reading		7/10	His written English
Writing		7/20	is still weak and
Spelling		Ab.	needs more effort.
Composition		11/20	
Written English			
Arithmetic		Ab.	Has tried but
Mental		12/40	must concentrate
Mechanical	D		more.
Problems		Ab.	Philip must be
History		Ab.	helped to form a
Geography			regular habit of
Nature Study	C		punctuality.
Art	C		
Handwork & Needlework	C		
Music	C		
Physical Education			

Class Teacher...........   Headmistress... D. Beavan..

A = Well above average for this class. B = Above average for this class.
C = Average for this class. E = Well below average for this class.
C = Below average for this class.

These grades refer to progress and effort and are comparative
only within the child's own class.
School opens again at 8.55 a.m. on September 2nd 1957

--------------------(Tear off here please)--------------------
I have received School Report for term ending July 26th 1957

................................(Name of Child)
signed ....(Parent or Guardian)

Please sign this slip and return it to the Class Teacher

Headmistress   PRINCESS
Miss D. BEAVAN

Dear Mr & Mrs Ly...
report which was
I hope that you
suitably for being
careless.

Yours
D. Be...

Christian Brothers' Cru...
REPORT
Name P. Lynott ...... Cl...
Term...Christmas...   P.1...

Subject		Marks (10...)
Catechism		8
Irish:	Reading	7
	Writing	7
	Spelling	4
English	Reading	9
	Writing	8
	Spelling	6
'rithmetic		8
Drawing		6

Attendance.......................
Punctuality..................
Homework...................
Conduct...................

Signed. D.+.O. C...

Beannachtaí na Nollag
na lathbhana go ...
on Leanbh Íosa dú...

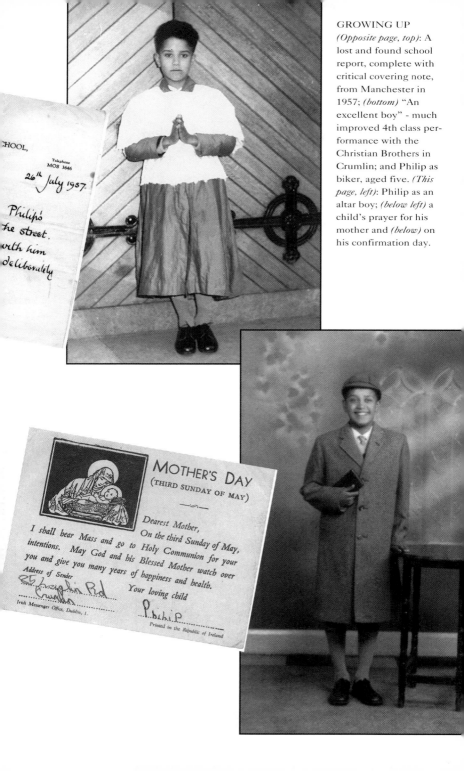

GROWING UP *(Opposite page, top)*: A lost and found school report, complete with critical covering note, from Manchester in 1957; *(bottom)* "An excellent boy" - much improved 4th class performance with the Christian Brothers in Crumlin; and Philip as biker, aged five. *(This page, left)*: Philip as an altar boy; *(below left)* a child's prayer for his mother and *(below)* on his confirmation day.

CHOOL,

Telephone
MOS 3646

26ᵗʰ July 1957.

Philip's
he street.
rth him
deliberately

MOTHER'S DAY
(THIRD SUNDAY OF MAY)

Dearest Mother,
On the third Sunday of May,
I shall hear Mass and go to Holy Communion for your
intentions. May God and his Blessed Mother watch over
you and give you many years of happiness and health.

Address of Sender
Crumlin Rd

Your loving child

Philip P.

Irish Messenger Office, Dublin, 1.

Printed in the Republic of Ireland

THE FIRST BAND: two shots of The Black Eagles from Crumlin when a rather bashful-looking Philip was 11 years old. The group's singer, it would be another couple of years before he took up the guitar.

SEEDS OF A LEGEND *(Anti-clockwise from top)*: a later Black Eagles line-up with Brian Downey second from right; Philip with musician friends including members of The Movement and Skid Row's Brush Shiels (second from left) and Nollaig Bridgeman (third from right); Philip, aged 20, with Philomena when she came to visit him at his first flat, in Clontarf, in 1969; and Thin Lizzy – Philip, Eric Bell and Brian Downey – with Philomena, outside The Clifton Grange Hotel in Manchester before the band boarded a rented van to head for London and the start of their first English tour.

THE YOUNG
DUDE: portrait of
Philip in the early
days of Thin Lizzy.

ME AND THE
BOYS *(Top to
bottom)*: Publicity
shot for the first
Thin Lizzy line-
up with Brian
Downey and
Eric Bell; the
classic mid-70s
'Live And
Dangerous' team
with Scott
Gorham and
Brian Robertson;
and Philip's last
band, Grand
Slam.

THIN LIZZY /phonogram 1976

HOLD THE FRONT PAGE: Philip and Bob Geldof, two Irish superstars at the end of the decade, ham it up for the cover of the 1979 Hot Press Yearbook.

LONESOME ON THE TRAIL: Philip gathers his thoughts around the campfire.

MY DA: Philip and Cathleen, aged 1 year.

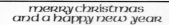
merry christmas
and a happy new year

philip, caro, sarah, cathleen, gnasher

FAMILY MAN *(Top to bottom)*:
Philip and Caroline on their wedding day, with Philomena, and
Jean and Leslie Crowther; Philip,
in Dennis The Menace jersey and
scarf, with Sarah and baby
Cathleen; season's greetings from
the Lynott family (and Gnasher
the dog); Philomena with her
grand-daughters; and Philip, Sarah
and Cathleen on holiday in
Marbella, the August before his
death.

CERTIFICATE FOR ORDINARY SHARES

MANCHESTER UNITED
FOOTBALL CLUB LIMITED
(INCORPORATED UNDER THE COMPANIES ACTS, 1862 TO 1900)

This is to Certify that PHILIP LYNOTT ESQ

is/are the Registered Holder(s) of FIVE HUNDRED*

Ordinary Shares of £1 each in the Company, subject to the Memorandum and Articles of Association thereof

Given under the Common Seal of the said Company

Exd

NOTE: NO TRANSFER OF ANY OF THE SHARES COMPRISED IN THIS CERTIFICATE WILL BE REGISTERED UNTIL THE CERTIFICATE HAS BEEN SURRENDERED TO THE COMPANY'S REGISTRARS, NATIONAL WESTMINSTER BANK LIMITED REGISTRAR'S DEPARTMENT. PO BOX 82, 37 BROAD STREET, BRISTOL BS99 7NH

CE/874/A/--

RED-BLOODED *(Clockwise from top)*: The certific
confirming Philip's shareholding in M.U.F.C.; with
pal, the great George Best; and with another Old
Trafford favourite - Philip's own caption, handwritt
on the back of the photograph, simply reads: "Steve
Coppell of Manchester United (my team)".

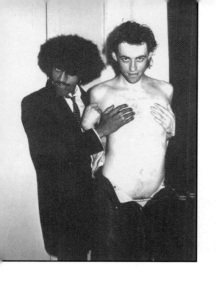

FAMOUS FRIENDS
(Anti-clockwise from above):
Philip with Marie Osmond
(his own caption reads "Me
and me girlfriend - Part1");
with Bob Geldof; with
Bono; and with the late
Peter Cooke.

ROCKER:
on the
live and
ous and hav-
all.

Pic: Colm Henry

Pic: Colm Henry

THE MAN IN BLACK

she'd be constantly worried about him. So, it was eventually agreed that the best solution all round would be for Philip to move out of the Crumlin house and live on his own. He and another guy moved into a lovely flat in Clontarf on the North side of Dublin with a superb panoramic view of Dublin Bay and with the majestic Dublin Mountains in the background. The song 'The Friendly Ranger At Clontarf Castle', on the first Thin Lizzy album, was inspired by the time he spent in this lovely part of the city. The palm trees which were planted just before Philip took up residence in that flat are still there, although now fully grown, of course.

One time, when we were over in Ireland, Philip invited Dennis, Percy, Roy and me to stay at the flat, an invitation which we happily accepted. No doubt it was part of my motherly instinct to want to find out if my young man was capable of taking care of himself while he was free of adult supervision. I was thinking how mature he'd become until, in the process of admiring the tidiness of the rooms, I inadvertently stumbled upon a cupboard where the two flatmates had, in obvious haste, hidden their rubbish in anticipation of our arrival. That discovery gave us all a good laugh!

On another trip to Dublin, he took me out to an Italian cafe near one of his favourite haunts, The Bailey pub off Grafton Street – it was probably the Coffee Inn, where he used to hang out quite a bit. I heard him asking the waiter, who obviously knew him, for, "My usual order but can you put it on two separate plates?" Two plates of piping hot Spaghetti Bolognese duly arrived and I spotted Philip slipping the waiter a half-crown (twelve and a half pence in today's money). My heart secretly went out to him when I realised how much he wanted to treat me to a nice meal – but that that was all the money he had left.

Of course, I felt sorry for him, and he was cute enough to know that such a gesture would soften me up. Sure enough, when we left the restaurant and he was basking in the glow of having bought me a meal, he asked me to treat him in return. I couldn't have resisted, even if I wanted to and so we went straight to the open-air Ivy Market where, after meticulous deliberation, he chose a 1930s-style gent's evening suit with long tails. The front was worn shiny with age, but that didn't matter – he was convinced it was the business. He also chose three or four shirts with detachable collars which would prove useful no matter in which direction fashion shifted. As soon as he could, he took the suit to the cleaners and I washed the shirts for him, and when I saw him all dolled up in the new gear I thought he looked marvellous.

In all, I spent about five pounds that day, a sizeable sum at that time, but it was worth every penny just to see his unrestrained delight with the purchases. I guessed that he must have been a regular customer at that market because I noticed that the old ladies there knew him very well, as did all the flower women on Grafton Street.

By now, Philip had become very conscious of his image. He was beginning to pay the kind of close attention to his clothes and to his appearance that is characteristic among rock stars. Not that he was a star yet. In fact in a way, his almost dandyish look reminded me of his father The Duke, who always dressed as well as funds would allow. Most of the time Philip looked the part and as he achieved greater success and affluence he could afford to wear pretty much exactly what he wanted to. Later in life, most fans probably thought of him as a really sharp dresser with a wardrobe always full of carefully-chosen clothes. But that wasn't always the case and I saw him several times, over the years, in a beautifully-tailored, expensive suit with a pair of cheap pumps on his feet!

I have to be honest and say that there are areas of Philip's life that remain a mystery even to me. We were great friends and, compared to most mother-son relationships, he was very honest and truthful with me. But the lengthy periods we spent apart meant that there would always be significant gaps. On the other hand, the occasions when we *could* be together were so precious to me that they remain ultra-vivid in my mind. For whatever reason, when Philip was around something out of the ordinary was bound to happen. It might seem odd to people who weren't around in the 1960s but these things often related to his unconventional appearance.

I remember when he was about seventeen or eighteen, Dennis and I invited him and his then girl-friend, Gale, to join us in Ibiza for what was his first real overseas holiday. He packed his clothes in a very shabby hold-all, which looked decidedly out of place beside my brand-new luggage. Before going for a spot of underwater swimming one day, he left this somewhat unsightly object on a sunbed which was in fact being used by another tourist. She turned out to be an insufferably overbearing woman. When she came back to the sunbed, she threw his bag on the ground in disgust and went on to harangue me when I began to offer an apology. Thankfully her tirade was abruptly interrupted by Philip's return from the beach – when she saw him with his big, bushy hairstyle, she fled! He had that effect on people at times.

Generally, I was only aware of Philip's various musical adventures in Dublin and all the changes in the various bands with whom he worked, through his regular phone calls and copies of newspaper clippings, since I was myself busy with my own hectic schedule running the Manchester hotel. Only gradually did I become aware of the depth of his determination and his burning desire to make it as a rock star. I missed a lot, as a mother, not being in a position to be with him all the time – and I guess that he missed a lot too, not having me around. Certainly, I will always regret not having been a first-hand witness of the goings-on of his teenage years, including his involvement with earlier bands like The Black Eagles, Skid Row and The Orphanage, and of course, the early Dublin days of Thin Lizzy. I know they can be desperately troublesome but there's a kind of tragic vulnerability about teenage boys and I'd like to have been in a better position to help Philip through these difficult years.

In a general sense, I knew that music had become the main focus of his life. I proudly read of him being voted as one of the top 20 Irish rock performers by the readers of an Irish pop magazine in 1968, when he was still in Skid Row. That poll, incidentally, also featured Brush Shiels and the late Rory Gallagher. I took a keen interest in how Thin Lizzy's first single, 'The Farmer', would do when it was released in Ireland, but little did I dream what it would ultimately lead to. After his departure from Skid Row, Philip had begun writing his own material, a comparatively rare activity in Ireland at that time, since up to then most bands – whether they were showbands, cabaret acts or even the more credible rock acts such as The Black Eagles – concentrated almost exclusively on cover versions of tunes by The Beatles and other chart acts of the time. Of the songs on Thin Lizzy's first LP, all bar one of them was written by Philip, no mean achievement for a man of just twenty-one years. In the context of his music, Philip Lynott's vivid freewheeling was at last given the free reign it had craved for so long, and he thrived on it.

The success of Jimi Hendrix, another flamboyant black musician with a liking for colourful clothes and progressive rock 'n' roll, must also have been a tremendous inspiration to Philip. The striking similarity between the two was later reflected in rumours that Philip was to play the part of Hendrix in a film. Obviously, it would have been very gratifying for me to have been a first-hand eye-witness at the birth of the rock'n'roll legends that Philip Lynott and Thin Lizzy were later to become. But there was great satisfaction to be derived, nevertheless, from the fact that my boy's reputation was growing. It wouldn't be long before Thin Lizzy – and Philip Lynott – would achieve lift-off.

While the musical revolution of the so-called swinging '60s had transformed the entertainment scene in Britain in a way that few could have thought possible even a decade before, the culture of official Ireland, even in the early 1970s, was still extremely conservative, buttoned-down and conventionally-minded. Musically, the domestic scene was dominated by the showbands, groups of eight or ten musicians in neat suits who played set routines comprising note-perfect versions of the latest British and American pop songs. At their height, there were as many as six hundred showbands travelling up and down the roads of Ireland, among them the likes of Dickie Rock and The Miami Showband, Brendan Bowyer and The Royal, and The Capitol Showband.

Such was the power that these outfits and their managers possessed, that all other types of music were effectively marginalised and frozen out to peripheral beat clubs and backstreet shebeens.

For the kind of original, progressive rock that Thin Lizzy wanted to pursue, as I understand it, there was little point in putting down permanent roots in Dublin. At that time, there was only one Irish radio station, the state-run Radio Éireann, whose musical policy was by and large restricted to light pop, easy listening music, Irish ballads and traditional Irish dance music. From what I can remember, the main outlets for live music were the dance-halls and ballrooms (which only used showbands), ballad sessions for Irish folk groups and variety shows which at best might have a ten minute spot by a pop group in the middle of all the comedians, jugglers and magicians. Most serious Irish rock fans had to listen to Radio Luxembourg to hear their favourite artists and their favourite songs.

Yet it is ironic to note that, even in the 1990s, despite the proliferation of radio stations throughout the country and the acclaim for artists like Thin Lizzy, The Cranberries, Van Morrison, Sinead O'Connor and U2 all over the world, young Irish rock bands have had to mount a public protest campaign because they still find it so difficult to have their music played on Irish radio. What a strange little country we are.

So, like many Irish artists before them – from The Bachelors to Rory Gallagher's Taste and Van Morrison's Them – Thin Lizzy moved to Britain in search of the career their own country could never offer them. Of course, not many of their predecessors had access to a hotel where they could stay and eat for little or nothing, and they were smart enough to stay with us in the hotel as often as was convenient. If they were gigging within driving distance, they would automatically head back to the Clifton Grange after the show. That gave me the welcome opportunity to keep an eye on them and ensure that they at least ate properly. They could eat and sleep and do their laundry in the hotel, an advantage enjoyed by very few bands at the time. So, in my own small way, I suppose I assisted Philip on the rocky road to rock stardom. As it happened, in the wake of the success of The Beatles, and the beat group explosion that followed, The Clifton Grange Hotel had become a regular stopping-off point for many of the country's hit-making groups: acts like The Searchers, The Troggs, The Bonzo Dog Doo-Dah Band, The Temperance Seven, The Flowerpot Men, The Ivy League, backing musicians for Val Doonican and Frankie Vaughan, and others who sadly failed to scale the dizzy heights of fame.

I remember one guest who was part of an act of identical twins. Believe it or not, it was Rick Parfitt, eventually to enjoy enormous success with Status Quo, and when Philip met him many years later, he remembered his time at The Biz. The hotel was a popular place for musicians to stay, partly because I had developed an understanding of their attitudes and the particular requirements of their profession, but it also had a great atmosphere. It was a fun place to stay and, in spite of shouldering the responsibility of running it, I have to admit that I enjoyed it enormously, particularly since most of the musicians who stayed with us were genuinely nice, down-to-earth if eccentric people, contrary to the public perception. We actively discouraged anyone who was difficult or unpleasant, but then that was hardly extraordinary. Sports stars such as Hurricane Higgins and George Best, who actually became a really good friend of ours, were also regulars, as indeed was Geoff Hughes, who played the part of Eddie Yates in *Coronation Street*. I was "Auntie Phyllis" to most of them, including "Bestie", as we knew him.

Philip loved football and he later told Liam Mackey, a journalist with *Hot Press* magazine, that he preferred his band's fan club to be known as the Thin Lizzy Supporters Club.

Brush Shiels had, in his own inimitable way, remained on good terms with Philip, even after Philip had been dumped from Skid Row. When

Brush was planning to get married, Philip knew he could not afford a proper honeymoon, so he persuaded me to invite Brush and his wife-to-be Margaret to stay in our hotel. As the hotel was fully booked out at the time, we improvised some mattresses on the floor for them, but at least they got away from Dublin for a half-decent honeymoon! The happy couple arrived wearing the most flamboyant clothes imaginable, in keeping with the hippy mood of the times, and I gave them a portable radio as a present.

During their stay, it happened that a member of The Ivy League, one of our regular guests, was suddenly taken ill, putting their next few gigs in doubt. Any cancellation would have meant them going without wages and they might not have been able to pay me for their rooms or food either. After some thought, I came up with a brainwave: I asked Brush if he would like to earn some money, and he jumped at the chance, gamely deputising for the stricken musician after some hasty rehearsals, even overcoming the inconvenience of having to use a borrowed guitar which was set up to be played by guitarists who played left-handed. Or so the legend goes!

Between one thing and another, I never got the chance to find out what his new wife Margaret thought of this rather unusual interruption to her honeymoon, but Brush still tells the story of him getting paid for a gig during his honeymoon, and I can vouch for it. Margaret and Brush have kept in touch with me – I always admired him for taking such good care of his own mother, whose death devastated him.

In many ways, I think life has been somewhat unfair to Brush. His talent is widely recognised but for my money he deserved far more recognition internationally than he received. He appears to have fallen foul of some of the more unscrupulous charlatans who inhabit the music industry at a vital time in his career, and never to have fully recovered the momentum with which he exploded onto the scene in the first place. While I'm on the subject of Brush, it's worth saying that, after Philip died, and I was suffering from grief on a terrible scale, some people were mischievously spreading rumours, and Brush somehow got the impression that I disliked him. A bit later on we talked it over and cleared the air. Some Irish people have a regrettable habit of spreading careless tales, often with no deliberate malice or understanding of the difficulties they may cause. This was a case in point, because I've never had anything but the highest regard for Brush.

The way in which he had helped out The Ivy League was typical of the carefree and eventful life that revolved around the hotel, and a by-product of our policy of only encouraging guests whose company we really liked. In a way, the Clifton Grange almost took on the character of a club, through which people made contacts and got to know everyone else who visited. The Radio Luxembourg DJ, David "Kid" Jensen was one of the first in the British media to show an appreciation for the music of Thin Lizzy. As a result, Philip used to stay with him in the Grand Duchy when he visited Radio Luxembourg. Jensen was largely responsible for the first Thin Lizzy album reaching the number one spot in the station's Hot Heavy Top 20 and so – needless to say – he was always a welcome face at the hotel.

As time passed, it made increasing sense for the Clifton Grange to concentrate, almost exclusively, on showbusiness clientele. Because showbusiness people generally work late and might go for a meal after completing their night's work, breakfast was a moveable feast, more likely to be set for midday than mid-morning, so it would have been inconvenient to have had guests with conflicting lifestyles. The hotel was often described at the time as one big show-business family. Most of the time, we had great fun, often sitting up into the small hours of the morning listening to one band telling us about how well they had gone down at their gig and another admitting they had died a death – although sometimes you knew the reality was the reverse. Such can be the insecurity of showbusiness; it's often hard to be absolutely sure what's for real and what's not.

Whenever Philip arrived, he would immediately renew his contact with

Percy. If there was a band staying at the hotel who had a record deal, he would pump them for information about their contract, their management set-up and other details. In his fascination with the whole music scene, he would often be first up and last to go to bed, always relishing the stories he heard from the various characters he chatted to. He was as cute as a fox, his ears always open for useful advice or information, and he would especially observe the various personality problems and conflicts inherent in any set up where there are four or five talented people competing for attention. He would note the number of times musicians would arrive with us as part of one group and leave as part of another. That early attention to business details explains why I never had any concerns about his ability to take care of himself financially in later years.

The music scene in the late 1960s had a reputation, which has inevitably intensified with the passing years, for fairly conspicuous drug use, but we did our best to keep a tight rein on such matters at The Biz. In view of the tragedy that overtook Philip later, I must quite categorically state that I never had any inkling that hard drugs were being used in the hotel at any time and I still believe that they weren't. In spite of, or maybe even because of, its illegality, pot was the most popular and trendiest drug at the time, and I must admit to having enjoyed it a few times myself, partly out of curiosity. I presumed that many of our guests regularly indulged in the privacy of their bedrooms and that wouldn't have been a major problem for me.

But anything harder was definitely out of the question as far as I was concerned, and anyone suspected of having any connection with hard drugs was made most unwelcome. The social climate of the time indicated that pot was okay, but I think there was a genuine fear of the harder stuff, and thankfully it just did not seem to intrude on our scene at all – though clearly it would have an appalling impact on Philip's life, and by extension on my own, in the longer run.

While I was generally quite innocent about drugs, I could usually detect from a person's shifty behaviour that they might be using something. I regularly came upon groups of musicians giggling and behaving oddly, and they would try to pretend there was nothing going on, but I was a little more aware than they suspected, and sometimes I would feign ignorance just to add to their hilarity! Some might see that relatively lax environment as having sown the seeds of Philip's later involvement with hard drugs, and they may even argue that, somehow, I should have prevented Philip setting off on the drug trail that was eventually to kill him. But, in showbusiness, the softer drugs like cannabis were assumed to be part and parcel of everyday life and I had no reason to assume that they had any long-term effects.

Besides, cannabis use was so prevalent among musicians that any attempt on my part to prevent Philip using pot when he was with me would not have prevented such a very determined and increasingly confident young man doing exactly as he pleased when he was out of my sight. I gave him the usual motherly talking-to about drugs and other matters before he moved permanently to London but, just like the rest of our showbiz guests, I knew he smoked pot now and then and I also knew there was little I could have done to stop him.

And when you think about it, for every casualty like Philip, there were hundreds and hundreds of people involved in rock 'n' roll and showbusiness who used cannabis and never went near heroin. What it is that takes people over that threshold I'll never know, but I really don't think that me confronting him about using cannabis would have made a blind bit of difference. Since he never lived with me in his adult life, in most respects I had almost as little influence over his lifestyle as I had on the other musicians passing through. The curious thing is that he often tried to persuade me to give up smoking cigarettes and drinking, and I did so once for a while, just to please him. He was probably the only man I ever obeyed!

By this stage, with the hotel going well, I was much more content in my life than at any time up to then. I was responsible for a successful business, in receipt of a regular income, secure in a stable relationship with Dennis, and taking enormous pleasure from observing Philip's enthusiasm for his increasingly successful music career. I was also proud of the fact that he had also become a very observant person, ever-vigilant about whatever was going on in the world about him.

As Philip's fans will be aware, many of those observations are evident in his lyrics and poems. As he drove along the motorway, or waited at an airport, an advertising hoarding might catch his eye and a phrase or an idea would go straight into the notebook he carried with him at all times. He was a highly intelligent young man of considerable depth, and possessed of a real creative drive. Even his own mother could see that!

'Whisky In The Jar', that brilliant ballad of passionate love and romantic highwaymen, has gone down in rock history as the single that first catapulted Thin Lizzy onto the world stage, but only die-hard fans know how close it came to not becoming a single at all. If it hadn't, who knows how different so many lives would have turned out?

The song was originally recorded as an impromptu filler track, merely to be used as the B-side of their next single. But to the band's initial displeasure, their label Decca Records insisted on making it the A-side. For once, you might say, someone in a record company got it right. Released in November 1972, 'Whisky In The Jar' got off to a slow start and did not enter the British singles chart until 20th January, 1973. As you can imagine, this was a tremendously exhilarating time for us and everyone in the hotel eagerly followed its progress as it moved slowly, week by week, up to the number six spot. God, it was wonderful to see this kind of success happen to your own son. In Ireland, it went to number one, of course, confirming the band as national heroes. I was really proud of Philip.

What made the feeling even better was the fact that it was a great record. To this day, I love the way 'Whisky In The Jar' opens with Eric

Bell's ringing electric guitar and Philip's distinctive voice howling out at you. I knew that Philip was writing good songs himself but the fact that this was an old Irish folk song appealed to me. Indeed, in 1993, I was delighted to hear it again on the soundtrack of Jim Sheridan's superb film, *In The Name Of The Father*, about the disgraceful injustices heaped on the Guildford Four by the British "justice" system. But I think we'd better not go into that here.

Before the release of 'Whisky In The Jar', of course, Thin Lizzy had recorded two other albums. The first, called *Thin Lizzy* was released in April '71, and the second, *Shades Of A Blue Orphanage*, in March '72 – this album has a cover photo of Philip, Brian Downey and Eric Bell walking through St. Stephen's Green in a typical Irish downpour. I love that picture – it captures not just the spirit of the era, but also Philip's love of Dublin, which is something that he never lost.

Neither album had sold well enough to enter the British charts, although they had been reasonably well received by the more discerning rock fans and had earned a solid reputation for the band all over Europe. However, as their career developed, the band had been to Germany to play club dates and to perform on German television.

In fact, to me, the boys seemed to be permanently busy, working nearly every night, whizzing all over Britain and Ireland for tours and festivals. Up to the time of that first album coming on the market, I had still been sending Philip the money I had promised when he first moved into his flat in Clontarf. Like most rock bands, they had often pretended to be more successful than they actually were, and gigs back in Ireland, where they were obviously far more popular, were initially used to subsidise some of their dates in Britain and on the Continent. Now that Philip no longer needed to be subsidised, I felt that things were beginning to move for them.

The first real confirmation I had that Thin Lizzy's career had taken off was the recording of a television programme Dennis and I attended in Manchester, in early '73. Lulu and an impeccably-dressed Joe Dolan, of all people, were also on the bill. When Thin Lizzy arrived at the hotel before the recording, I insisted that they each have a bath. I wanted them all to look spotless for this important appearance on national television. Needless to say, my fussing and mothering gave them a good laugh.

At the time, Philip used to wear what I can only describe as a disgusting woolly Rastafarian-type hat. I suppose you could say that it was in keeping with the new untidy style of the time. To me, it was more like a tea-cosy, with his hair poking through the various holes in it. Anyway, that afternoon, I washed their clothes and ironed their jeans, much to their disgust, since it was considered old-fashioned then for men to wear a crease in their trousers, and I darned all the holes in Philip's ugly hat.

So when the band came on the studio set to perform 'Whisky In The Jar', which was hitting the charts by then, I was really proud to see the son for whom I had walked the streets, trying to find work in order to clothe and feed him, up there in front of the cameras. There he was, with a record in the charts and starring on television with his band. Even noticing that the hat on which I had done such a thorough repair job during the afternoon now had as many holes in it as ever didn't faze me! They obviously thought of me as a boring, old-fashioned mother, whereas they wanted to portray a devil-may-care, hip image. And judging by the reaction in the studio at the time, I could only conclude that they'd got it right.

It was equally exciting for me, attending my first real Thin Lizzy gig, when they supported Slade for what must have been their debut Manchester concert, at the Free Trade Hall. Slade were so popular that the streets were full of police and the kids all wore hats reading, 'I'm Slayed'. Slade had a reputation for attracting a skinhead audience with racist tendencies, and when we arrived backstage before the concert, I noticed Philip and the band were very nervous about the ordeal ahead.

When Suzi Quatro finished her set, we took our seats just in time to see Lizzy arrive on stage. They were greeted by a chorus of abuse, with louts shouting slogans like "Get off the stage, black arse" and "Get back to Africa." I wasn't used to the intense atmosphere at concerts and the air of barely controlled tension. I reacted emotionally, attempting to run over towards where some of the most vociferous offenders in the audience were gathered. I shudder to think what might have happened if Dennis and my friends hadn't succeeded in restraining me – those guys looked thoroughly nasty and I doubt if they'd have been intimidated by a middle-aged woman losing her temper. Philip, meanwhile, was pleading with the audience in his broad Irish accent, "Ah, come on, give us a chance, just give us a chance." Somehow, his pleas got through and most of the audience listened, but I think the band were relieved when their spot was over and they could retreat to their refuge backstage, bruised but not broken.

That night, we threw a party at the Clifton Grange and decorated the place with balloons and promotional material supplied by the record companies. Suzi, Noddy Holder and Philip were there, with the other members of the band and they had a great time together. Needless to say, there wasn't even a hint of the unpleasant racism evident in the audience – my own impression was that Noddy Holder was a very decent fellow.

About a year later, Thin Lizzy were back at Manchester Free Trade Hall – only this time, they were top of the bill. It was a wonderfully memorable night for me. It began with a police escort through the centre of Manchester in the limousine Philip had arranged for us – but that was just the start of it. Lizzy had deliberately reserved a space in the centre balcony for me and my fifty personal guests. I felt like the queen, being able to preside over such a brilliant occasion.

It was an astonishing gig, like nothing I had ever seen in my life before. By this stage Lizzy had put together a real show, using amazing lights, and there were loud explosions from their smoke bombs that frightened the life out of me – I thought they were real bombs, because there was a lot of violence in Northern Ireland at the time, and there was always the threat of bombing in England as a spill-over from the Northern troubles. Needless to say, the crowd, who were more used to that kind of thing, went berserk – the band went down so well that I lost count of the encores. I remember being struck at the time by how *loud* the music was – it took three days for my hearing to recover, but that didn't matter. It was the start of my love affair with heavy rock.

What a turn-around it was, when you think about it, for a band to play a venue in front of a bunch of mindless racist hecklers one year, and the next to be greeted with the kind of hysteria I thought was reserved only for The Beatles and The Rolling Stones. Thin Lizzy's growing stature was even bestowing some reflected glory on me, as people arrived in Manchester to seek out 'Phyllis' place' because of the Lizzy connection.

As their success grew, I took advantage of the occasional opportunity to snatch a glimpse of the inner workings of the record industry. I was taken to meet a chap called Frank Rogers at Thin Lizzy's record company Decca, and I was terribly impressed at seeing a real gold disc on the office walls there! Decca were a very big record company – they had many famous hit artists on their books such as Vera Lynn, The Bachelors from Ireland, Mantovani, David Whitfield, Lonnie Donegan, Tommy Steele, Billy Fury and Dickie Valentine, most of whose music I had heard on the radio and liked quite a lot. When I looked at the gold records by some of these celebrities adorning the Decca offices, I was struck by the possibility that, before too long, my own son and his band might be joining such an elite collection.

Frank was a brother of the Irish singer, Clodagh Rogers, who had had hit records with some nice pop tunes such as 'Come Back And Shake Me' and 'Goodnight Midnight'. The fact that I admired her and her music, and that they were both Irish, helped break the ice and I really got to like Frank almost immediately. I have to admit that being part of all this made me feel just a little bit special. How many other rock 'n' roll stars' mums were happily admitted to the inner circle? But I was very privileged that that was the kind of close relationship I had with Philip.

There were other occasions when I would be called upon to help out over one problem or another, because I got on so well with most of the band members, the management and crew. For example, at one stage an acrimonious row developed during a tour of Germany and the situation became so critical that the group were on the verge of splitting up. Their management company, led by Chris Morrison and Chris O'Donnell, had bought the band's contract from Ted Carroll and they relied on me a lot in those days. So, when there was trouble brewing in the camp, they pleaded with me to fly out to Germany, at their expense, in an effort to keep the group together.

Fortunately, the disagreement – whatever the cause of it – was resolved and my flight was unnecessary, but the occasion proved how tenuous the survival of a band often is. When one considers the clash of personalities and the inevitable squabbles that arise when people have to spend so much time together, often working under intense pressure in strange circumstances, you could argue that it's a miracle that rock bands last as *long* as they do. Needless to say, Thin Lizzy was no more exempt from such traumas than any other band on the road. Far from it.

When I originally queried Philip about the kind of people who were looking after his music business interests, he reassured me that the 'two Chrises' were two genuinely nice guys who attended church every Sunday. He jokingly promised me that the day they stopped going to Mass, he would start worrying about them.

Of course I knew that was just a load of old baloney – but overall I had the feeling that Thin Lizzy were in good hands. There was a bit of an anti-climax after 'Whisky In The Jar', but that's not altogether unusual, and overall they were making good progress. From my perspective as a mother, Thin Lizzy's spiral of success was so overwhelming that I hardly had time to reflect on it, as one highly-publicised incident was swiftly followed by another. Philip regularly sent me pre-release acetates of new records, but I was probably too close to him in a personal sense to appreciate fully how popular they were becoming all over the world. Sometimes one of their songs would come on the car radio and I would nearly crash with excitement, particularly when I reflected on all we had been through, together and separately, and how we were now enjoying the fruits of our separate careers.

My own life had settled down to the kind of contentment unimaginable when we were evicted from the Catholic Home in Selly Oak. Racial abuse was something I now encountered rarely. I never allowed it to affect me anyway, always putting it down to a combination of fear and ignorance. I have always freely associated with black people, and proudly number several of them among my closest friends, including Roy and Percy, who was like a son to me, and who became a regular guest in my Dublin home in the grief-stricken years that were to follow Philip's death. When they wrote to me, they would sign their letters: 'Your son'. Percy often referred to me endearingly as his 'Irish Mammy'.

Because Philip was now abroad a lot, touring and promoting his records, I was not aware of him having to deal with overt racism, but I believed he was sufficiently strong to cope with it in his own way. Some of his best friends, like Percy and Roy, were black, yet he played in a white rock group. Not surprisingly, it was sometimes impossible for me to distinguish the real events of Philip's life from the inevitable hype that surrounds celebrities in all walks of life, and probably even more so in the flamboyant, anything-goes rock business.

There was the occasion when he was shot at in America, for instance. The first I learned of it was when he rang to warn me that the media would probably be reporting it, and he wanted me to know he was safe. Naturally I was extremely shocked and upset, and even now I have no idea what was going on at the time or what the real background to the incident was.

There were also the now-famous stories of him allegedly going deaf with tinnitus, stories which, to my knowledge, were totally without foundation and which Philip claimed had originally been dreamed up by a record company publicist as a publicity stunt. Whatever the truth of the matter, I could not avoid becoming extremely concerned, especially when television companies ran programmes about the dangers of loud rock music, using Philip's alleged problems as part of the evidence to support the theory. But, of course, such publicity served to enhance the image of a band eager to portray themselves as taking major risks by playing dangerously loud for the sake of their music. And maybe in that perverse way, it was somehow good for the band. For an outsider, it can be deeply disturbing to see not just the lengths people have to go to to achieve success, but also to realise that this kind of media manipulation actually works.

Another blast of publicity which did my own nerves absolutely no good at all centred around a violent incident in a bar. Supposedly, Philip was just talking to a girl who had asked for an autograph. Whatever was going on, her guy obviously didn't see it that way and smashed a pint glass over Philip's head, with the result that all the Lizzy roadies piled in and created a dreadful ruckus. Afterwards, he phoned me to warn me that the media were going to run stories along the lines of: "Lynott loses an eye in bar-room brawl." He wanted me to know that there was no foundation to the speculation. Again, looking back, I have no idea to what extent the Lizzy PR machine had actually fed the media a line and it suited the newspapers to run with it. I do believe that Philip himself was conscious of the possibility that these kind of bad-boys-of-rock stories might benefit the band, but I was never fully sure to what extent his calls were merely bravado or truthful re-assurances.

Philip was astute enough to realise that the comparative novelty of a black Irishman was another exploitable angle with obvious media appeal, and he was capable of cleverly using his colour to good advantage as part of the band's and his own image. But at the same time, he was unquestionably genuinely proud of his Irishness.

Every year, he would endeavour to be at Clifton Grange for our annual Saint Patrick's Day party which would inevitably turn out to be a real humdinger and at which George Best and other celebrities were regular, and boisterous, revellers.

On a trip to New York, he bumped into a New York cop, who was amazed to find that that this tall black guy had such a thick Irish accent.

Philip phoned me afterwards asking me to send the guy a complimentary T-shirt and a copy of his first collection of poetry. In due course, the cop became one of his best friends in America.

When Philip's first book of poetry was published, I, like a lot of other people, including some of the hippest rock critics, was pleasantly surprised and enormously proud. Until then, it was unusual for a songwriter in a heavy-rock band to have poetic ambitions, but when you explore Philip's song lyrics, it becomes apparent the extent to which his work transcends the run-of-the-mill rock song. I got the lovely feeling reading the book that I was entering into Philip's world and sharing in his inner life. The songs, teeming as they are with numerous references to Ireland, Dublin, his friends, and aspects of Irish culture and history, seem to me to possess a genuine poetic flair.

I have to admit that it was only after his death that I began to study his poems and lyrics in depth, and slowly began to understand the extent to which his lyrical work bore a direct relationship with his life. I regretted not listening to them more attentively during his life and exploring their deeper meaning with him – but I must say that it's one of the problems with the kind of hard rock that Thin Lizzy played. At times it's so difficult to make out what's going on in the songs that I do think, in Philip's case at least, a lot was lost as a result.

One of the things that does come through in the songs is that Philip loved Ireland. He never felt in any way alienated from the ordinary people of Ireland, despite being black and having been born in England to an unmarried Catholic mother. I have often suppressed a wry grin when I hear people winning prizes in quizzes by wrongly answering 'Ireland' or 'Dublin' to the question, 'Where was Philip Lynott born?'. But irrespective of the *place* of his birth, Philip always regarded himself as Irish and was deeply proud of Ireland and his Irishness throughout his life. It must have added a real sense of achievement for him that someone from an underprivileged background in Dublin could compete with the best the music world had to offer. I suppose a significant number of the world's most successful rock stars do come from deprived, working-class backgrounds, underlining the extent to which great talents are undoubtedly lost in other areas of human endeavour. Because one of the great things about rock 'n' roll is that it does offer an escape route for working class kids with artistic leanings. Sadly, it's one of the few.

GLORY DAYS – PASSING BY

"Then somewhere from the north
This Gale I knew just blew in
and I am afraid."
– from 'Look What The Wind Blew In' by Philip Lynott

When Philip, then still in his teens, moved into his first flat in Clontarf in Dublin, he had a girlfriend called Gale. I am reasonably certain that she ended up staying in the flat with him, although she would discreetly move out whenever I came to visit Philip.

I can't say I'd have been utterly shocked if I'd known, but there's no doubt that it was a typically unconventional thing to do at the time. In those days in Dublin, it was rare for couples to be as open and frank about their sexual affairs as they might be in the Ireland of the 1990s. Today, a very high percentage of households might have at least one person in a sexual relationship outside marriage. But the widespread scale of this is quite a recent development.

The extent to which young people had sexual experiences in Ireland was generally much rarer in those days as well. Before Philip moved to London, I would have assumed he was probably less experienced sexually than a young person would be in similar circumstances today – as indeed I had been when I left Dublin. But perhaps not. Between my departure from Ireland and Philip's move to Dublin, the 60s revolution had occurred and had resulted in enormous worldwide changes in young people's attitudes towards sexual morals. Ireland had not escaped those influences.

Television had become a fact of Irish life by the mid-1960s. Teilifís Éireann had been launched with great fanfare at the end of 1961, and was now broadcasting five or six hours a day, of which well over 50% featured programmes brought in from abroad, mainly America. Gradually, even on home-produced programmes such as Gay Byrne's ground-breaking *Late Late Show*, matters relating to sexuality were being more openly discussed. At last, there were signs that the Irish people were beginning to shake off the stifling fears and anxieties of Catholic repression.

We had been so cushioned from the realities of life during my own pre-television, teenage years, that when I emigrated I had no knowledge of a lot of issues that today dominate the news and the magazine programmes – issues like homosexuality, for example, or abortion. Philip and I were probably quite similar in that we both underwent a process of awakening after we left home. It is, I suppose, a necessary process and, if it's well managed, a very beneficial one.

Looking back now, I suspect that the main reason for him wanting to have his own flat originally was that he was beginning to build relationships with girls, and there were definite limits to how far he could go while under his Granny's watchful eye in Crumlin! Apart from the morals of it, the house was too small and offered little in the way of the privacy you might need for even the most innocent sexual exploration. In Clontarf, he was obviously free of those restrictions and it must have been shortly after his move there that he met a young, green-eyed beauty called Gale. It must also have been around that time that he wrote 'Look What The Wind Blew In', a song which appeared on the first Thin Lizzy album, and in which he sings: *"Then somewhere from the north this Gale I knew just blew in."* In the printed poem version of the song, the word *'Gale'* has a capital letter, whereas obviously, if the word were being used as simply indicating a 'wind', it would require no capital letter.

Philip and Gale were to enjoy a very close relationship for about six years, living together in a cosy flat in Embassy House at the junction of Cleve Road and West End Lane in London. At one point, they were engaged to be married, a fact very few people know – I remember her selecting a ring costing £4 in a second-hand shop, a poignant image when you put it in the context of the scale of Thin Lizzy's later success and the amount of money Philip made.

I thought Gale was a fabulous person and both Dennis and I worshipped her. She was the highly intelligent daughter of a dentist from Northern

Ireland and had three lovely sisters. We loved her company so much that she often came on holidays with myself and Dennis to places like Ibiza. She had a strong personality and was always perfectly capable of holding her own on every level with Philip. Although they would have their occasional rows, they were very much in love and he seemed very fulfilled by their relationship. When he had moved to London, she moved over with him and she often came to stay with me in the hotel in Manchester. Despite their being together for six years, she refused any suggestion that they might have a baby together unless they were married first. And in the context of what happened later, I'm convinced she was right.

After they had enjoyed a steady relationship for about five years or more, she told me she was unhappy about the direction in which they were going. By that stage, Thin Lizzy had become quite popular and Philip was becoming a big star in his own right. That level of celebrity in itself brings its own pressures and temptations, since it usually attracts the opposite sex in droves, like bees to a honeypot, such is our perpetual fascination with fame.

Since I was busy in Manchester and he was in London when not travelling extensively with the band, I was hardly in a position to know how he was behaving one way or another. As far as I could tell at the time, both he and Brian Downey, who lived near him, in Greencroft Gardens, and who had an Irish girlfriend called Terry, were in steady partnerships. I was not so naive as to assume that Philip was a saint, and I did know that he would not want me to find out if he stepped out of line, because he knew of my high regard for Gale.

In retrospect, I have no reason to imagine that Philip did not respond willingly to the increased sexual availability of young woman attracted to him as a rock star. Gale certainly suspected he was beginning to have extra-curricular relationships of one kind or another and this was leading inevitably to frequent, unpleasant arguments. So, she felt a break from him for about six months, during which she would go travelling abroad, might clarify his true feelings and help make up his mind as to whether he was sufficiently committed to her or not.

"After all," as I said to her, "if you go away for a while and it turns out that he doesn't miss you, then at least you'll know where you stand." I told her that I loved her dearly and that I would understand and support her no matter what decision she came to. I was really on her side in the matter, as I was disappointed by Philip's attitude.

While she was away, Philip moved out of the London flat into a rented house. When Gale came back, I pointed out to him that she now had nowhere to live, and so she moved into what had been their flat on her own. From a sexual point of view, it seemed Philip wanted to have Gale around when it suited him, but he also, unfairly, wanted his freedom to have other women too, even though Gale had stuck with him when they struggled to live on cans of beans and virtually nothing else.

I have to admit that his attitudes were clearly contradictory and somewhat chauvinist. He would complain to me if any of his "spies" reported that she had been meeting any other male friends. He often became extremely upset at the thought that she might take a fancy to other men, whereas he wanted to play around with no restrictions. His behaviour really irritated me and I remember even at one point suggesting to Gale that she should investigate whether she could sue him for breach of promise. I wasn't often critical of Philip but in this instance I was so enraged by his attitude that I think I would have given evidence against him in court!

But Gale was too proud to go down that road and, much to my deep regret, she faded out of his life. Although they remained friends right up to his death, inevitably Gale found a new man, whom she later married. She also carved out a very successful career for herself with Sky TV. I know that a mother has no hold over her children in this respect, and it was probably a selfish reaction on my part, but I was extremely upset when I lost her as a future daughter-in-law – just so that Philip could play the field and enjoy the rock 'n' roll lifestyle with what were probably groupies and hangers-on a lot of the time.

As her parents had passed away, Gale had no family in Ireland and she often referred to me as 'Mother'. I'm happy to say that she married a lovely man called Colin and they have two children, Zoe and Jamie. They all stay with me in my house on their regular visits to Ireland. Like they say, true friendships never die.

I suppose I knew that, in the long run, Philip would develop a curiosity about the absence of a father in his life. It happens in most single-parent families – some choose to tell their children as little as possible but I never felt that that would be fair. A child has, I believe, a right to know and so I had decided to keep him as fully informed as possible. As time went by, I filled in as many of the missing pieces as I thought he could handle.

Of course, I couldn't help fretting and wondering whether not having a father made him feel odd when he saw that nearly all his school pals had so-called 'normal' families. When he was still young, I explained to him the background to his birth, convinced him that his Dad loved us both and had wanted to marry me – and I told him that Cecil had since married a nice lady, whom he introduced me to at a dance, and that he was raising a family of his own. I never wanted to badmouth his father or to make Philip feel that he was somehow unworthy.

I never really held anything back from him in this regard, but it didn't seemed to preoccupy him too much either, perhaps because his upbring-ing was so full with all the people in Ma's house and he was part of the gang in what was a busy neighbourhood. On the face of it at least, Philip just got on with his own life. In the meantime, I also let Cecil get on with *his* life and we had been totally out of contact, more or less, since the court hearing.

When Philip was about ten, he asked me a lot of questions about his Dad. Then he enquired if I would forward a letter he had written to Cecil. I said yes, because I didn't see any way that I could refuse – but I later decided, unknown to Philip, not to post that letter. It was not an easy decision for me to be deceitful to Philip, but I knew that Cecil was happi-ly married with a family of his own, and I thought that such a letter from Philip might arouse old feelings in him, or even cause some discomfort to his wife and family. I'm not saying that that was the right decision but I felt it was at the time. To put it simply, I suppose I reasoned that it was best to leave well enough alone. Because, quite genuinely, to have met Cecil might have had a hugely disruptive effect on a boy who was happy at the time. But it is still a tough call for any mother or father to have to make and my heart goes out to anyone who faces that particular dilemma.

I knew deep down in my heart that, sooner or later, curiosity would almost certainly get the better of Philip's apparent indifference and that he would want to meet his Dad face to face. I had resolved that if he wanted it, I would be wrong to obstruct him in something so important – but the older he was at the time, the better he'd be able to handle any emotional turmoil that might be involved. And so it transpired – genuinely, there was no rush on it from Philip's side.

Some time after the release of the Thin Lizzy album *Fighting*, in 1975, a popular magazine – some might classify it as a scandal sheet – called *Titbits*, published a rather fanciful article about Philip, emblazoned with the headline, "The Lizzy In A Tizzy About His Dad!" Cecil's wife accidentally spotted it and drew it to his attention saying, "I think this is about your son."

When Cecil read it, he went straight down to the Thin Lizzy management office and spoke to Chris Morrison – and announced there and then that he was Philip's father. Philip was recording at the time in Soho, I think. The people in Philip's management office were perplexed as to how to deal with this new drama, so when they telephoned me for my advice, I asked them not to put Cecil in touch with Philip until I had thought the matter through and spoken directly to Cecil myself. After all, I had no way of knowing if Philip, by now a grown man, actually wanted to meet his father, at this late stage. Would he want whatever illusions or mystique he had built up to be shattered? And might he interpret – or misinterpret – Cecil's interest in meeting him as being merely a product of his success as a musician?

I was just beginning to mull things over when the phone rang and I was amazed to hear Cecil's voice. He was calling from the management office. I recognised his voice straight away, despite the fact that we hadn't spoken for years. He asked if I could arrange for him to meet his son and I just couldn't refuse. I then confirmed to the office that this man was indeed Philip's dad. After a series of phone-calls back and forth, during which my heart was doing a crazy dance inside me, a meeting between them was arranged for the following evening. I offered to accompany Philip if he felt he would like someone there, but he quite firmly and confidently said, "No Ma, I'm grown-up enough to do this on my own." He promised to phone me after the meeting to tell me how it had gone.

Next evening I was waiting anxiously and impatiently by the telephone, yet no call came through from Philip. I was simultaneously furious with him and concerned that the meeting might have gone badly. It was classic Philip. He was an incurable romantic and could be extremely solicitous – but he could also be thoughtless and forgetful. When I eventually could hold off no longer, I rang the office to be told that he was still engrossed in a recording session and had skipped the meeting. I knew this must have been bitterly disappointing for Cecil, but a second appointment was made.

This time, Philip did show up. I don't know how he was feeling at the time but I'd have assumed that his first meeting as an adult with his natural father would have been a momentous occasion for him. Maybe he didn't take to Cecil, or they just didn't really know what to say to one another after all those years, but he seemed far less excited afterwards than I had expected him to be. I rationalised this to myself, concluding that they were now two adult men with utterly different lifestyles and attitudes, and with very little, if anything, in common, and that was probably about the size of it. At the very least we can conclude that Philip Parris Lynott wasn't very impressed with Cecil Parris – and maybe, just maybe, the feeling was mutual.

That day Philip met not only his father but also Cecil's wife and their daughter, and his sister Sarah, who had also come along. One can imagine that such an encounter must have been quite trying for all concerned, and there may have been a sense in which this inhibited the possibilty of any kind of in-depth discussion between the two central characters in the drama. I have often wondered whether, had Philip not lived the whirl-wind life of a rock star, he might have had more time to get to know his father more intimately, and perhaps explored his father's background, political views, culture and so on.

But these are not things that can be forced by anybody – such relation-ships must grow naturally or not at all. As it transpired, Philip rarely men-tioned his father after that meeting and, as far as I know, that was the only time they ever spoke face to face.

Who can really guess what went on in the minds or hearts of either of them?

Although I always loved my son dearly, and he was rarely far from my thoughts at any stage in my life, I could not help observing a marked change in Philip's personality over the years as he became more success-ful, more powerful and more affluent. Particularly as a result of all the tor-ment we went through together when he was a child, as a mother I still find it difficult to be really critical of him – but there would be no point in denying that he had his share of failings like any other human being and that these could be exaggerated by the circumstances of his life. Yes, he was romantic and generous and sentimental, but an unpleasant and unnecessary aggression sometimes crept into his manner, more particular-ly towards the latter part of his life.

Some people have suggested that that change in his personality was a direct result of his use of cocaine, but I had no way of knowing that then and I can't say that I know it for certain even now. I did notice him begin-ning to talk very sharply to people and, because I did not like what I saw,

I pulled him up on it many times. He didn't argue when I scolded him, and afterwards, I would remind myself that I often behaved likewise under the pressure of the moment and I too would need to apologise later. But the bottom line was that I didn't like to see him treating people badly, no matter who they were. And if he was capable of doing it while his disapproving mother was around, was it not probable that he was behaving even more boorishly when there was no-one to answer to except the flunkies and yes-people who inhabit the fringes of the rock world?

My old friend Percy had encouraged Philip to project the more aggressive side of his nature, which he felt the fans would respond to very positively, and while in commercial terms he may have been right, there is a possibility that such posturing only served to allow a more unpleasant side of Philip's character to assert itself. Not that he had undergone a Dr. Jekyll and Mr. Hyde-like transformation. I firmly believe that Philip was more consistently generous and attentive to me in his adult life than many sons are to their mothers. Dennis and I were taken on various Thin Lizzy tours overseas and treated like royalty. We had a very good relationship with the band members in general, and it was a terrific treat for Philomena Lynott, from working-class Crumlin, to be taken free of charge to stay in some of the most luxurious hotels in the world and to meet countless world-famous celebrities. I often had to pinch myself to confirm that it was really happening. We shared many close, fun times together, all of which have become even more precious and memorable to me since he passed on.

There was no way that Philip was mean or miserly with his money. He enjoyed spending it having a good time with his friends – like the time he invited nearly 300 guests, among them Bob Geldof, Graham Parker and other stars, to his lavish 28th birthday party, in 1977, amid the immense grandeur of Castletown House, in Celbridge, County Kildare. He would also have thoroughly enjoyed being invited to be a judge for the Miss World event in 1978 – that wasn't something he'd have had any inhibitions about. He was generally happiest when he was partying and he had very little of the introspective artist about him.

He was one of a select number of celebrities invited on Virgin Atlantic's inaugural London-New York flight and he later featured in advertisements for Virgin Atlantic and Maxell tapes, which were useful at least in bringing the money rolling in. And despite the fame, adulation and wealth, he had an endearing ability to laugh at himself. Once when we shared an Aer Lingus plane-trip after he had achieved a degree of celebrity, he began laughing aloud at an article in their in-flight magazine which listed him in a chart of the worst-dressed men. He loved all that and, in my opinion, probably played up to it, and I took enormous satisfaction in seeing that he never seemed to allow any of that fame to erode his sense of humour. In moments like that I felt that he had, early on in his career, learned the happy knack of separating the real Philip Lynott from the star and that he successfully kept the different personae separate most of the time, though certainly not all.

He often complained that the combination of his skin colour, his big, bushy, black hairstyle, his gangling, six-feet two-inch frame and his very individual stride – all difficult to disguise or hide, I think you'll agree – meant that he could never become inconspicuous in public. And it was true. Unlike other rock-stars who can – and do – become anonymous by wearing different clothes or a wig or some disguise, he could never really escape so easily.

When Dennis and I arrived back in Dublin one afternoon after a tour of the Irish countryside, we immediately spotted a distinctive figure walking along the pavement as we drove up O'Connell Street – it was Philip. On another occasion, I went to the Brown Thomas store in Dublin's fashionable Grafton Street to buy him a black stetson hat which I knew he would really appreciate. I asked the elderly shop-lady for the largest hat in stock because of his hairstyle. When I rejected the one she first offered, she insisted that there was no larger size available and began to look at her colleague pityingly, as if the hat must be for a retarded person with an abnormal head. It was only while taking my name for a special order that she realised the hat was for Philip, a regular customer, she told me, whose measurements she had already!

In a small but vivid way, that illustrates how difficult it had become for him to maintain any real sense of privacy as his reputation grew, and I know he craved, just occasionally, to become anonymous and to melt into the crowd. But if the hat doesn't fit, I guess you can't possibly wear it!

After all the racial abuse we had endured when he was younger, he now occasionally had to deal with people who saw us together on the street thinking we were dating and muttering equally outrageous insults. One of the worst instances I can remember occurred when I took him to visit the dentist. Afterwards, Philip was suffering the effects of the anaesthetic and as we walked out from the dentist's residence, I had to hold him up because he was so groggy. Even when I managed to get him into a cafe to take refuge, I could hear the unkind tongues wagging, expounding on their crass misunderstanding of the situation. But we never made any attempt to hide or apologise for our closeness, and he once described our relationship as more brother and sister than mother and son, so some people inevitably got the wrong idea. That might have been avoided had an obvious father-figure been around, but what the hell! The fact that we loved each other was much more important than any slings and arrows that narrow-minded busybodies might throw at us.

Although Philip became an astute businessman who was very conscious of the need not to be short-changed in an industry where sharks flourish, I never felt him to be unduly money-conscious. He knew when someone was not pulling his or her weight for the band, and he would openly remonstrate in no uncertain terms because he wanted everyone associated with Thin Lizzy to be as committed as he was. And there were rows, with Eric Bell, Gary Moore and Brian Robertson in particular – occasions when egos clashed and the future direction of the band had to be sorted out. But the point is that Philip was the leader and the creative focus of Thin Lizzy, and while I am certainly not saying that he was always right, in the end there can only be one leader.

But in my experience he was neither greedy nor a hoarder of pointless possessions. Nor was he ever attracted to worthless possessions merely to impress others or to excite envy. He was not one for wearing ostentatious jewellery, diamond rings or Rolex watches to show off. He had no flash car, for example, and never learned to drive. Plain pieces of silver attracted him. Gadgets also fascinated him and he enjoyed picking up an unusual bargain. He would proudly show me some watch that you could use underwater and do all sorts of fancy things with, and then he would admit it had cost a mere £13.

In London, or on trips overseas, he would tend to wear more outrageous fashion, but he would be less ostentatious back in Dublin, partly because there is something in the Irish character that reacts against that kind of behaviour. Whenever he returned to Ireland, he was conscious of the possibility of meeting old friends who might not be doing so well, and he was always careful not to make them feel that they were missing out. Nor did he ever try to disguise his broad Dublin accent, because he would always identify with the genuine down-to-earth Dubliner and, in some ways, getting back to those people was his way of maintaining contact with his real roots.

Such contacts may have provided him with the best opportunity he had of fading into the background for a while. Of course, when asked, he would frankly admit to thoroughly enjoying fame, and there is an inherent contradiction in this enjoyment and his desire to be able to escape from it when it suited him. He remarked to me, on more than one occasion: "When we were kids, didn't we all want to grow up to be famous, and aren't I lucky to have been one of the few granted that wish?"

On balance, I suppose he did revel in being the star, but he also harboured an inherent suspicion of the falseness inherent in fame. And, as I say, he could always relate to the everyday, hard-working guy or girl, and their dreams and ambitions.

In the end it's fair to say that I generally thought that he was very down-to-earth, though others may have felt otherwise. One of his so-called friends accused Philip of being so vain that he would walk up Grafton Street in Dublin constantly looking at his reflection in the shop-windows. But I do that myself. Who hasn't? And either way, it's hardly a major crime, is it?

If Philip thoroughly enjoyed being the star, Philomena Lynott equally enjoyed being the mother of the star. If he was a notorious party animal, then I enjoyed that side of the life too – it'd be dishonest and hypocritical of me to suggest otherwise. And the truth is that when Philip had the opportunity, he treated me amazingly well, inviting me to tour with the band whenever I was free to. And I loved it.

In 1974, along with Brian Robertson from Glasgow, a young Californian called Scott Gorham had joined Lizzy. Those who know Lizzy's music will be aware that they operated as twin guitarists, replacing Eric Bell with a new and distinctive sound after his departure. It was the patented Thin Lizzy style which would mark the band's greatest records and bring them to the brink of megastardom. On one of the band's U.S. tours, Scott introduced Dennis and me to his wealthy parents. They in turn invited us to be their guests, and to stay in their breathtakingly beautiful home in the mountains around Hollywood, surrounded by many of the mansions that Scott's father, a master builder, had built. My eyes were attracted to a magnificent coffee-table which they casually informed me had cost $10,000. Well, hello! I liked both parents and we got on well with them. They were so phenomenally rich that they could fly virtually anywhere by private plane at a mere whim. Needless to say, all that wealth and privi-lege had somewhat spoiled Scott, who would regale me with stories about all the famous old film stars, like Red Skelton, who were regular house guests when he was growing up.

When Scott had originally announced his intention of moving to

Europe, his disapproving father had given him a wad of money and told Scott not to expect any more hand-outs from him. Obviously, the elder Gorham had worked hard to earn his fortune and did not appreciate the possibility that Scott might be turning his back on all that to adopt the rock 'n' roll lifestyle. Thankfully, Scott was successful enough not to have to feel embarrassed about the career he'd chosen, and he was a lovely, warm, genuine guy – in fact the general camaraderie between Scott and the various diverse personalities around the band was a key factor in making touring with Thin Lizzy a bundle of fun.

Being on tours, particularly in the USA, made me realise what a mammoth task it is putting a major rock band on the road, with so many people involved, and with trucks, limos, sound gear, lighting equipment, merchandise, promotional material and so on, not to mention the complex business of hotel bookings, media interviews, personal appearances and a thousand and one big and small problems all to consider if the show is to be successful.

One of the highlights of my travels with the band came during a visit to Chicago for a major concert. On arrival at O'Hare airport, I naturally headed towards the luggage carousel to collect my bags. When Philip told me that all of our luggage would be taken care of by somebody else, I could hardly believe him. To me, this was the height of luxury, not having to worry about such normal chores as taking care of one's baggage. But that was only the start of it!

Immediately upon entering Chicago's Hyatt Regency Hotel, the first sensation I experienced was the scent of expensive perfume wafting up from the luxurious carpets. Even the porters were magnificently attired and walked with a very stately bearing. Or that was how I perceived them, anyway. After showing Dennis and I to our sumptuous room right next to Philip's, the porter stood stiffly to attention with his hands as good as outstretched for a tip. Unfortunately, having just arrived directly from the airport after our flight from England, we didn't even have a dime between us. So he turned and walked out in disgust, much to our embarrassment as the guests of a rich celebrity!

I was preoccupied with taking in the opulence and the dizzying view out over the city when someone came and discreetly placed packages on either side of our bed. When Dennis opened them he discovered an ounce of dope in each package! In a panic, Dennis ran down to Philip, who nonchalantly explained that the stuff was meant for some other room, not ours. But whose room? That was the unasked, and therefore unanswered, $64,000 question.

That night, the record company drove us in elegant stretch limousines to a top-quality Mexican restaurant. Soon the tequilas were being distributed and, amid the goings-on, I spotted Philip and the rest of the band larking about and trying to make me laugh while an overweight Mexican in an enormous sombrero was trying to serenade me. Philip then departed for some pre-arranged television and radio interviews, while we were next whisked off to a huge theatre for a Genesis gig. Unfortunately, jetlag was finally catching up on me and I suspect that I may have fallen asleep during their set. But it had been a wonderful night all round.

Dennis and I travelled the length and breadth of America, to such places as Maryland, Washington, Las Vegas, Galveston, Miami and Atlanta. And, as I said, we loved every moment of it. On our way through Maryland, we took the opportunity to visit my sister, Irene, who lived there with her husband, Don. Then, when we reached Los Angeles, we went in search of our friend Georgie Best who was living in the USA by then, his English League days behind him. As it happened, he was not at his house when we called, but we found the place occupied by his friend Bobby McAlinden, another legendary footballer. He kindly asked us in and invited us to make ourselves at home, told us there was beer in the fridge and left us to our own devices. Sometime later, when Georgie himself telephoned the house, he was amazed to hear the voice of his "Auntie Phyllis" on the line.

When George came back, he took us out to Fat Face Fenner's Saloon, on Hermosa Beach, and we then transferred into a hotel right next to the beach. For our entire four-week stay in LA, we socialised nearly every night with Bestie and his friends and we had great crack. When Philip arrived in Los Angeles, he checked into a hotel on Sunset Boulevard and sent a limousine to take Dennis and myself to meet him. As we rode in this beautiful chauffeur-driven limo through the LA traffic, passers-by would stop and stare into the car. On such occasions, I could not help reflecting on how my new lifestyle contrasted with my early days in an oppressive English work-house. Would you blame me for enjoying myself, now that the good times were well and truly rolling? I certainly never felt any pangs of guilt – and why would I?

In 1977, Thin Lizzy undertook an extensive tour of the USA, supporting Queen for more than 40 shows. The tour had begun in disaster – the night before the band were due to travel to the States, Brian Robertson had become involved in a brawl in the Speakeasy in London with fellow Scotsman Frankie Miller. Robertson was rushed from the premises with his hand pumping blood and there was no way he could travel. In fact the verdict was that he would be unlikely to play again for a couple of months, having ripped tendons in his hand. Cancelling the tour would have been a desperate blow. Luckily, Gary Moore was free and sufficiently familiar with the Lizzy scheme of things to be able to slot into Robertson's place – and so it was onwards and upwards, for the moment at least.

Philip took me on board on this occasion as well, and I remember being whisked to a post-concert party in Los Angeles at which I met the late Freddie Mercury and Brian May, with whom Philip got on particularly well. The guests included a huge variety of celebrities such as Alice Cooper and Errol Flynn's daughter – all surrounded by burly security guards armed with guns.

Before arriving at the party, Philip gave us all strict instructions to drink nothing except from cans we opened ourselves. He insisted that rather than leaving a can down, even for a moment merely to visit the bathroom, we must take our drinks with us to avoid anyone putting foreign substances into them while we were away. His concern was heightened by the tragic death of a drummer in a band he knew, apparently as a result of something someone had slipped into his drink in similar circumstances.

No matter where you looked at this party you could see incredible glamour, but Philip was unimpressed with Hollywood – or with this taste of it anyway. "They're all plastic," he said dismissively. When I later spotted the biggest roll of dollars I had ever seen lying unattended on the floor, my eyes popped and I picked it up and handed it to a security guard – who swiftly stuffed it into his pocket as if finding the owner was not going to be his number one priority.

Not surprisingly, the pressures of touring – and let's be honest, the lifestyle surrounding life on the road – wreaked havoc on Philip's health. In an incident which in some ways presaged the circumstances of his death, he took ill with hepatitis during the tour and the final leg had to be blown out. It was regarded by business insiders as a mortal blow to Thin Lizzy's prospects of breaking America big-time. Finishing this tour, they might have pushed the album they were promoting into the higher reaches of the charts. But it was not to be.

Hepatitis is a horrible, debilitating infection and, as a result, most of the following album, called *Johnny The Fox*, was written while Philip was recuperating. Shortly after he began his hospitalisation, I took advantage of one of my visits to play a practical joke on him which I'm glad to say he enjoyed as much as those involved in the prank did. Knowing only too well at this stage how keen an eye he had for an attractive girl, I roped the hospital Matron and three beautiful young women, who were friends of mine, into my scheme. The girls were identical looking and performed in a cabaret group as Looking Glass – I asked the Matron to fit them out in nurse's uniforms, and she duly obliged.

As I sat by Philip's bed, I pretended not to notice when the first girl, Cindy, came in and did a bit of tidying up around the bed. When she left, Philip was clearly agog at seeing such a stunner. Next came Yvonne on the pretext of asking Philip for some piece of information for his wall-chart. Once more, Philip could hardly believe that the hospital had not one but two extremely attractive nurses who, it would seem, were likely to be working on his floor. Then the third girl, Valerie, came in and when Philip saw her he was absolutely flabbergasted. Before he had time to figure out that something might be going on, "Nurse" Valerie said she needed to examine his private parts. At that, we could keep the pretence up no longer and we all collapsed in a heap of laughter, including Philip!

There were also more threatening risks which came as part and parcel of the rock tour lifestyle. In August 1978, while in Memphis, USA, Philip was shot at by the irate driver of a car with which his own car, driven by his chauffeur, had been involved in a minor accident. Several shots were fired during a ten-mile chase through the streets but, fortunately, none hit either Philip or the car. In June 1980, he was detained overnight in Southampton General Hospital for treatment to a damaged eye, after a glass was thrown at him while he was signing autographs following a concert at The Southampton Gaumont – not the kind of news you want to receive about your son a couple of months before your second grand-child is due.

Fortunately, the eye was not permanently damaged and, in typical rock business style, the incident was used for publicity purposes. It was in Philip's nature to turn such events into jokes anyway, and I can remember him making fun of the whole episode by crawling around on the ground pretending to look for his "missing" eye.

But those rare difficulties apart, I loved every second I spent travelling with the band, and I will always appreciate the opportunity I had of seeing so many fascinating people and exotic places because of Thin Lizzy's success.

LOVE AND MARRIAGE

Gale and Philip were still living together in the Embassy House flat when he started his relationship with Caroline Crowther. As far as I know, he met Caroline at a party organised by the well-known Thin Lizzy publicist, Tony Brainsby. At that time, she was working in Brainsby's office, and someone from the Thin Lizzy office had escorted her to the party. He may have known her beforehand but it was on Philip's arm that she left that night, and that, as I understand, was how their relationship began.

It would be unfair to imply that Caroline stole Philip from Gale. I think, looking back, that the time may really have been right for him to move on – and Caroline clearly was the woman he wanted to move on with.

My first awareness of her came through one of Philip's almost daily phone-calls, when he happily announced that he had a new girlfriend. I distinctly recall him laughing as he told me that she did not have dark hair and green eyes like both Gale and I had – a reference to his habit of joking that he would only marry a girl who had both of these attributes.

I was a little stumped for a response to the news, partly because it most likely sounded the death-knell for his relationship with Gale, but I accepted that his new partner must be important to him since he was taking the trouble to tell me about her. And so it proved. Another phone-call, some time after that, brought the news that his new woman was pregnant, although there was no mention of marriage at this time. Of course, given my own history, I was hardly in a position to lecture him on that issue – even if I had felt that there was something inappropriate involved.

I met Caroline personally for the first time in the house in Anson Road in the Cricklewood part of London, which I believe Philip must have rented while Gale was away, and which was full of lively young people. I could not help wondering to myself whether or not Gale still hankered after Philip and if she would be hurt by the latest turn of events. But with Caroline expecting Philip's first child, I realised there was no foreseeable way back into his life for the long-time girlfriend towards whom I still felt a deep loyalty.

Caroline was a tall, willowy blonde, born into what you could describe as a conservative if hardly entirely conventional English family. She was very different in both appearance and personality to Gale, and I was sufficiently worldly-wise to accept that Philip would make his own choices. Nor would I accept that the turn of events fostered any ill-will in me towards the woman who was going to bear my first grand-child. I was, I admit, confused by the fact that, not only was I going to be a grandmother for the first time, but the woman who was carrying my son's child was still very much a stranger to me and a recent and unexpected arrival in my life.

While I was probably instinctively sympathetic to her, having a baby out of wedlock as I had done, there was some comfort in knowing that her circumstances were certainly nothing like as deplorable as mine had been. The father of her baby was with her and he was quite flush, if hardly secure, by this time. There was no likelihood that she would have to suffer the torment and the pressures I had endured – Caroline's own background was also far more affluent than mine had been, and in such matters as education and job opportunities, she was in a higher league than I could ever have realistically aspired to. But the fact that there might be stormy waters up ahead for Philip, for Caroline and for their daughter-to-be, could not be discounted. My only role would be to help all three of them in whatever small way I could.

After we got to know each other a little, Caroline invited me to her parents' house in London for tea. There, I met her father Leslie Crowther, the well-known television personality and presenter of shows such as *The*

Price Is Right, her mother Jean and the family. They were very respectable, eminently friendly people, they made a lovely fuss over me and we all got on very well together. She was the third of five children and, on various occasions, I met her brother, Nicholas, and her sisters, Charlotte, Lindsay and Elizabeth.

Caroline later told me of an incident which occurred early in her relationship with Philip, but prior to her introducing him to her family. One night, she took a cab driven by a black – or at least, dark-skinned – man to her parents' house. When Leslie saw the cab arrive, he noticed the driver and, assuming it had to be the new boyfriend Caroline had told him about, he came out and greeted him most effusively, shaking his hand and inviting him into the house for a drink. It was only the cabbie's astonished reaction that made him realise his embarrassing mistake!

In later years, he was reported to have made some very offensive remarks about Philip, but I think they were always meant as harmless jokes. Anyway, he was always courteous to me whenever I met him and I found it difficult to accept that the views ascribed to him by the tabloid press actually represented his true feelings.

As Caroline was having my grand-child I wanted to make a fuss of her too, so I took her on several shopping expeditions and treated her. We got on very well at that time and seemed to enjoy each other's company, so that part of the equation seemed to fit. Soon afterwards, Philip bought the house known as the Walled Cottage, at 184 Kew Road, Richmond in Surrey. I was a regular visitor there, sometimes giving Caroline driving lessons in my car. When he was away, she would sometimes visit us in Manchester and life for all of us proceeded calmly towards the birth of his first child, whom Philip was adamant must be born in Ireland and raised as a Catholic. Despite my own disenchantment with Christian society in general, I welcomed his strong views on these issues since they indicated that he was taking his impending fatherhood seriously, and that he saw Ireland as his real home.

As I have already mentioned, Ireland always loomed large in Philip's life. References to the country are scattered throughout his music, even as far back as the debut Thin Lizzy album, which contains titles like 'The Friendly Ranger At Clontarf Castle' and 'Eire', and a song entitled 'Dublin' appeared on their first EP New Day. 'Fool's Gold' on the *Johnny The Fox* album refers to the Irish Famine, which was hardly on the agenda at the time, though it's been hotly debated more recently. Apart from those references to the Dublin that he knew from his own experience, he developed a deep interest in Irish mythology, and that in turn fuelled his friendship with the artist Jim Fitzpatrick, whose highly elaborate and distinctive designs inspired by Celtic mythology adorned some of Thin Lizzy's most memorable album covers and posters.

His view of Ireland, though it had a Republican tinge, was heroic and romantic rather than political. Like most of us, he loved the Irish community and felt at home among the Irish people, and he would have kept himself reasonably informed on the political turmoil in which his adopted country was engulfed, but I never really probed his private political leanings. What was not in doubt at all was his yearning for all of us to settle eventually in Ireland when his days as a rock star were over, preferably in the Dublin he wrote about in the eponymous song, or the city he lovingly portrayed in *Shades Of A Blue Orphanage*. Perhaps the first step towards realising that ambition came when, towards the end of her pregnancy, he persuaded Caroline to stay with his friends Gus and Maeve Curtis and family in their house, Glyde Cottage, on the magnificent Hill of Howth, which overlooks Dublin Bay.

Caroline, a non-Catholic, had already begun taking instruction in the Catholic faith from a priest attached to Richmond Parish Church in London where Philip often attended Sunday mass, and where they planned to get married – but, as far as I know, she did not formally convert. To describe Philip as deeply religious would be misleading, but he was certainly God-fearing, no doubt on account of his Irish education which was far less liberal than a similar education today.

On his death-bed, in his final hours, Philip was to request the presence of a priest, and I don't think he could be accused of being hypocritical in doing so. At the worst, you could say that he was hedging his bets as he had always done.

Caroline had agreed that their offspring would be baptised into the Roman Catholic faith, and, in fairness to her, that promise was fulfilled after both children were born. She also deferred to his desire to have the baby born in Ireland, and while she was staying in the Curtis household, he arranged for her to look around for a suitable permanent family home for them in Ireland. In a million years, I could not have envisaged the fluctuating periods of contentment and turmoil, from one extreme to its opposite, which that house would bring to all of us.

"When you came into my life, you changed my world
My Sarah . . .
You are all I need to live
My love to you I'll always give."
– from 'Sarah' by Philip Lynott

With the birth of their first baby not too far off, Caroline attended an auction where she purchased for £130,000 a house known as Glen Corr, near Howth, a popular coastal resort north of Dublin. It's a cosy bungalow with a lovely garden, surrounded by protective trees and pleasant greenery, on a quiet road sandwiched between the Dublin-Howth railway line and the beach. Later, it was claimed that she could have acquired the property for £90,000 as there was only one other bidder present at auction and there was even a suggestion that he may not have been genuine – but this kind of gossip-mongering is easy to start and far harder to substantiate. Property-owners in the locality were said to have rejoiced at her purchasing the house for such an unexpectedly high price, but the fact is that she was only 19 years of age, pregnant and living in a strange culture. In that light, it was probably unfair of Philip – bordering on recklessness – to have given her the responsibility of attending the sale with a blank cheque-book.

The fact that, unknown to me at that time, there was already widespread drug abuse within Philip's circle of friends, business acquaintances and hangers-on may also have encouraged a kind of dismissive casualness in relation to money and other matters on Philip's part – although I was not to learn of his own serious involvement with drugs until much later.

Despite the price paid for the house, the expenditure did not stop there, and more money subsequently had to be spent treating it for dry-rot and rectifying other problems. It wasn't exactly a money-pit, but it certainly proved to be a substantial investment.

When her time came, I collected Caroline at Glen Corr and drove her to Holles Street Maternity Hospital in central Dublin. En route, I stopped to furnish myself with a plentiful supply of foodstuffs as I planned to stay with her in the hospital overnight, and then spoke by phone to Philip, who had arranged to fly in from London.

He arrived in an excited rush direct from the airport, taking the stairs in the hospital two at a time, but his anxiety had not affected his playful sense of humour. As he leaped past a hospital worker scrubbing the stairs, she looked up and said, "Hey, don't I know you? Aren't you somebody famous?" When Philip replied, "Yes, I'm Red Hurley," she said, "That's right. How's it goin', Red?". How anyone could have mistaken a tall, thin, black man like Philip for Red Hurley, a decidedly white, red-haired, male cabaret singer, is beyond me, but it satisfied the woman, who probably got a buzz from meeting a celebrity no matter who she thought it was.

Reassured that the birth was not likely to occur for some hours, Philip insisted on treating me to dinner at Jury's Hotel, where we accidentally – I assume – bumped into Frank Murray and the gang. Philip came in for a lot of slagging along the lines of, "Hey, Philip, I've just seen three camels and three wise men heading for Holles Street hospital!" (Christmas 1978 was only about a week away) and the good-natured banter from his friends helped him to relax.

Prior to Caroline's move to Ireland, Philip had confidently boasted that he was going to have a son, hence the irreverent teasing – but his sheer delight was apparent when he came out of the ward lovingly hugging his first child, a beautiful healthy daughter. When Caroline passed in a wheel-chair on her way back to her room, she burst into tears because she felt Philip was disappointed by her not giving him a son. But his adoring behaviour, then and later, was proof of his devotion to his daughter, and the next time I saw them together they were busily selecting a name, opting for Sarah Philomena in honour of his grandmother and mother respectively.

Money was not a problem for Philip by this stage. He owned the house in Kew in London, the Embassy House flat, also in London, Glen Corr in Dublin, and a little later he bought me White Horses, for my fiftieth birthday, a house which is situated on Strand Road, Howth, not far from Glen Corr and from the Sutton cemetery where his body lies today. But to keep the money flowing in he had to work extremely hard.

Philip still shouldered the lion's share of the responsibilities for the band – a fact that is often overlooked – writing the songs, working on the production, dealing with the management and the record companies, tour planning and, since he was the lead vocalist and principal songwriter, he was also the preferred target for most media interviews.

So, despite the purchase of Glen Corr and his intention that the children would be reared there (not to mention his fervent wish that, in time, he might himself retire there too), Philip spent comparatively little time at the house because he had to maintain London as his business base. There were too few opportunities for him to get back to his wife and child. He visited as often as his work commitments allowed, I'm sure, but never as often as he, or we, would have wished.

While Caroline was pregnant with their second child, I suggested to Philip, half in jest, I suppose, but probably wholly in earnest as well, that it was time that he and Caroline got married. So, when plans for the wedding were announced, I was genuinely happy for them and had my dreams of Philip eventually settling down as a family man renewed.

I can still recall a newspaper article at the time in which the journalist wondered what Leslie Crowther thought of his public-school educated daughter marrying a black, illegitimate, Irish rock star. That angered me. I wondered why the question was being asked about what Leslie Crowther thought of the marriage, and not what Phyllis Lynott thought? All of the press speculation centred on Philip's suitability as a potential son-in-law, but never on how good a daughter-in-law Caroline might be.

Leslie was also reported to have made an offensive remark about Caroline at a Variety Club lunch, allegedly quipping that when Philip asked for Caroline's hand in marriage, he replied, "Well you've had everything else" – a reference to the fact that they had already been sleeping together. In fairness, it was also reported that Leslie had phoned Philip to apologise but, given the nature of the publicity that celebrities constantly attract, there may be scant truth in either report.

Inevitably, there was considerable press publicity about the forthcoming wedding, with few reporters failing to remind their readers that they already had a 14-month old child, that Caroline had been fined £200 for possession of drugs, that she had posed nude for a girlie magazine, had worked as a topless waitress in Soho and was now pregnant with their second child. As if any of that was news worth bothering with, either way.

Like many mothers, I cried more than a few tears when I saw my son and his bride kneeling at the altar in the Saint Elizabeth Of Portugal Church, in Richmond, on St Valentine's Day, 14th February 1980. As with most marriage ceremonies, it was a happy, emotional occasion and I was proud to have so many of my friends present. And yet, as is so often the case, silly things intrude. On the way out of the church after the ceremony, the pair of new shoes I had purchased especially for the big occasion were cutting into my feet and giving me a lot of grief. As I walked alongside Leslie Crowther, I confided to him how my shoes were "killing" me and how I would love to just fling them off to relieve my feet. Leslie is genuinely witty and he took my mind off my problem by cracking a couple of jokes which made us both laugh. There are many photographs taken that day which caught that moment, with the two of us looking so jolly together – and which thankfully do not reveal the torment I was suffering over those new shoes! Looking back, I can only think how stupid I was taking the risk of ruining the day for myself by wearing a pair of shoes I hadn't even broken in and yet this kind of thing probably happens all the time to people who are trying to look as swish as they can for the big day. Maybe wedding invitations should carry a government health warning!

Scott Gorham performed the role of Best Man. He and Philip were great friends and shared a similar sense of humour and attitudes about a lot of things. Later, at the reception which was held in the Kensington Hilton hotel, I asked Leslie what he thought of the marriage and he astonished me by his somewhat off-hand comment: "Oh, it's taken a while to get that one off my hands." He may have meant it as a little joke to lighten the mood, but I was surprised by what I instinctively detected as a level of seriousness in his voice.

Philip and Caroline honeymooned in Rio de Janeiro, Brazil, while I took care of Sarah in the Kew house, content in my illusion that we all would live happily after.

I really didn't know until quite late in the day that Philip had been using hard drugs – which I always believe to be a mug's game. The first serious inkling for most of us, outside of Philip's inner working circle and the hangers-on at his house in Kew Road, Richmond, had come via a telephone call from Caroline alerting me to the fact that there were likely to be stories all over the media concerning a drug raid by policemen from the British Special Patrol Group on their house, at 8am on 13th November 1979. Apparently, the police had gained admission to the house at dawn, convincingly disguised as gas board workers and accompanied by two sniffer dogs. They later claimed to have found two quantities of cocaine in a jacket beside Philip's bed, some cannabis in the Mercedes car that he owned and was driven around in, and a cannabis plant growing in the conservatory.

At Kingston Crown Court, Philip, who was represented by George Carman Q C, claimed he had given up drugs completely since Sarah's birth. One of the band's former roadies helpfully admitted that some of the drugs may have been his.

I was particularly disturbed by the presence of cocaine, irrespective of who owned it, but my queries were dismissed by Philip's insistence that he and some others had tried cocaine once, merely as an experiment, and that the raid was a total over-reaction by the police to a non-existent problem. Whatever the truth, he got off – but, whatever way you cut it, Philip was lucky to escape a jail sentence.

The police had, by this time, earned an unpleasant reputation for harassing rock stars for drug offences, and they were not beneath planting evidence in some cases, so it had become difficult to know what exactly was going on in such situations. High-profile stars like ex-Beatle Paul McCartney, Keith Richard of The Rolling Stones and Pete Townshend of The Who had openly admitted to having indulged in drugs of one kind of another, but there was no reason to assume that every single rock star was on drugs and Philip's denial convinced me. The realisation that he might have developed a lethal drug habit did not hit me until it was far too late.

I suppose there must have been some inkling that all was not well at the back of my mind when he was busted a second time for possession of drugs at Dublin Airport, on his arrival on a flight into Ireland in May 1985. Some incriminating needles were alleged to have been discovered in his suitcase. His explanation on this occasion was that he had grabbed the first suitcase he found when hastily packing for the flight, and that the one he had chosen must have belonged to one of the numerous people who passed in and out of his London home. He was cleared by Justice Gillian Hussey, vehemently denied any culpability, and I had no option but to believe my own son.

But looking back now, I have to admit that I was being naive or gullible – or both. It had surprised and disconcerted me somewhat that, after the court hearing, he dashed back to England without stopping off to visit any of us in Howth. I probably excused his hasty flight at the time by assuming that he wanted to escape from a media pack ever-anxious for any scandal involving celebrities and drugs, or that he was embarrassed about the case among his Dublin friends – but I realise now, sadly, that I might have been simply trying very hard to avoid accepting the grim reality that was slowly creeping up on me – and, more lethally, on him.

My reaction was not helped by my own vast ignorance of the insidious nature of heavy drugs and my misplaced, motherly confidence in Philip's ability to avoid doing anything so stupid as to use cocaine or heroin. I had constantly warned him about the dangers of addictive drugs in the early days of the band and, later, I recall him admitting on more than one occasion that he had more or less tried them all, was not interested in any of them, and he implored me to stop bothering him about the subject. I never had any reason to say to him, "Philip, I do not believe you," and I am not sure whether I would have had the courage to do so either.

I was later to learn that he was so determined to ensure that I would never discover the depth of his problem that he had warned all around him never to breathe a word about it to me, and when Philip laid down the law like that among his inner circle, he really intended it to be obeyed. All of the lads knew that I had not the slightest suspicion of the extent of his drug problem. He knew I would be horrified by such revelations and would probably go berserk. In the event, I never got the chance.

Even when he was living in Glen Corr, he lived a mainly night-time existence and probably did all his dealing in the night-spots while I was innocently asleep upstairs, or over at White Horses. After a late night around the Dublin nightclubs, his friends would join him next day in the master bedroom where he watched a lot of television. I would always knock, out of respect, before entering the room and that probably gave him sufficient time to cover up anything he did not wish me to see. In hindsight, I knew deep down that something sinister was going on and I now have to live with the consequences of my own naiveté.

I eventually realised why, whenever we went on holidays with the children, he would arrange a suite for me and the two girls, while he had his own separate bedroom which he kept very private.

When Grand Slam, his next band after Lizzy, were rehearsing in a Community Centre near my home in Howth for their 1984 tour, everybody must have been under the strictest orders not to let anything slip about his drug habits to me. There was a report that during a row, one of the musicians threatened to tell me everything, but nobody did, and I continued in ignorance. Here is one case which very definitely contradicts the proverb that "ignorance is bliss."

Of course, it has been relatively easy, particularly with the benefit of hindsight, to put forward the argument that some of those who claimed to be his friends should have had the courage to tell me, or to do something to alert somebody about the deteriorating situation. Unfortunately, anyone who knew Philip well will vouch for the fact that he was a determined, strong-willed person, and that he would have been fiercely intolerant of the merest hint of disloyalty. Maybe that control is a characteristic of the drug-abuser, an instinctive means of protecting their habit.

It is possible to interpret the song 'Fighting My Way Back' on the 1975 album *Fighting* as either a prophetic warning of troubles ahead or as a track about a battle, even then, against drug-dependency. Other songs, like 'Opium Trail' and 'Sugar Blues' on the *Bad Reputation* (1977) album, have obvious drug inferences, as does 'Got To Give It Up' on *Black Rose* (1979). Philip himself claimed that the song 'Warriors' on 1976's *Jailbreak* album was about heavy drug users, and he sometimes talked almost in tones of hero-worship about people like Jimi Hendrix and Duane Allman making conscious decisions to see how far they could go. But it is always difficult to know how much of that attitude was an image for the media, exaggerated macho talk, or the truth. Perhaps, in a way, it's a bit of all three.

I must also concede the possibility that others close to him may have suffered from the same drug dependence. Some may now have to rest uneasy at night with the uncomfortable thought that they might have contributed indirectly to his sad demise, by helping him to keep his addiction a secret from those who were not dependent, and who might have have done something about it.

By some bizarre twist of logic, Philip did not want to tolerate having anyone else around him who might have a dependency on any drug, even alcohol. It seems outrageous now, and more than a little hypocritical too, but he once asked me to inform the parents of Thin Lizzy guitarist, Brian Robertson (or Robbo as he was known), that their son had a drink problem. For all I know, Philip may have suspected that Brian had a drug problem too and wanted to have that sorted out, but it defies logic that he would have been so concerned about another's addiction and done so little about his own.

On one occasion, I was told that he had actually struck a roadie by the name of Studs in anger – with an umbrella of all things! – when he found traces of marijuana in the house, after he had been left to caretake it while Philip was away. Perhaps, since it was his band, he may have felt a responsibility to those involved, especially if they were younger, like Robbo and Studs. However, it's more likely that, in this instance, he was conscious that it could have been the police rather than himself, who discovered the drug traces.

I noticed during this time that Philip was putting on a lot of weight and it did not suit him. I had always assumed that a serious drug habit would have had the opposite effect, that a junkie becomes haggard and gaunt, so I merely thought he was losing interest in his appearance. He had developed a particular fondness for Courvoisier brandy and a tendency to drink quickly, but other than that, I noticed no tell-tale signs of strange behaviour. Admittedly, I would only see him for three or four days at a stretch and then he'd be gone, so I could not be aware of his every move or anything like it. You reach a point where your interest in the minutiae of someone else's career or their daily life diminishes, and you simply allow them to get on with it. And besides, there wasn't any great new ground being broken either. After Lizzy split, Philip did some good solo work, but I couldn't tell you even now whether or not he did solo gigs after the demise of Thin Lizzy.

I had to accept that he had work to do, to earn his livelihood, support his family and whatever musicians were in tow, and I had to give him the space to do so. No member of a rock band wants a mother, no matter how well-intentioned, fussing around all the time, interfering in things she knows little about. Through my experience in the hotel trade, I was accustomed to having a lot of people around me but I was also used to allowing them the privacy they needed.

By this stage, I was in effect acting as the de facto housekeeper there, and I have to emphasise that there was never any evidence of hard drugs in Glen Corr, but at that time my attention was fully occupied taking care of Dennis, Philip, and any of the band members or their wives who stayed with us. Their lifestyle allowed them to sit up through the night, but I would be exhausted from cooking, cleaning, ironing and other daily household chores.

They may of course have indulged in all sorts of drugs behind my back, but Philip never once used a hard drug in my presence. Not once.

Caroline has also had her own problems with drugs, but to give her credit, she had the discipline and determination to overcome them. I can recall a visit she and her mother made to Dublin, during which the three of us went for a meal in the King Sitric restaurant near Howth. During the meal, Caroline excused herself and when she returned to our table she was noticeably drowsy. Jean Crowther had to take her home. The explanation I received subsequently was that her new contact lenses were hurting her eyes, and, in my innocence, I swallowed that story, but Jean was obviously less naive than I and was more aware of what was happening. During a later visit to the Crowther house, she made a remark to me to the effect that she was taking care of hers and I should take care of mine. Although her words stirred something in me, I did not think to ask her to explain them more fully. I was too innocent or stupid or out of touch to comprehend that she was gently trying to alert me to a major problem of which I was totally unaware. Had I responded to her comments, maybe subsequent events would have taken a much different turn. Unfortunately, all of our lives contain so many 'could haves' and 'if onlys', not least mine.

In due course, I learned that Caroline, who was fined by the courts for possession of cannabis, had courageously taken the crucial step of admitting her problems to her family and was receiving counselling for her alcohol and drug problems. I even accompanied her to a drug counselling clinic in Bristol, without ever suspecting for a moment that Philip might need similar attention.

When these developments led me again to ask relevant questions of Philip, he vehemently repeated his denials, told me that he wasn't using hard drugs, and since I had always believed he would never lie to me over a serious matter, I accepted his word completely. Whenever I found him staying on in bed in Kew, I presumed he had either been out partying or working late in the studio. The fact that those who knew the truth, and the seriousness of the situation, conspired to avoid telling me, only added to my exclusion, and I don't mind saying that it took me a long time to forgive them. Equally, some will argue that it was not their responsibility to become informers since, after all, society has little time for those who tell tales behind another's back.

BLOOD ON THE TRACKS

"But my home is where my heart is
And my heart is not at home."
– from 'Sweet Marie' by Philip Lynott

ooking back it can be hard to piece all the memories together. To
what extent am I still blacking things out, my mind playing whatever
tricks it has to, to give me stability as I try to come to terms with the grief
over Philip's death? To what extent was I, at the time, deliberately not
acknowledging something that I must have felt in my heart of hearts?
Sometimes I think I must have been a fool not to have copped on. Other
times I ask myself, how could I have known? And then I recall that as far
back as 1980, Caroline was having problems with drugs to an extent that
put her relationship with Philip under terrible strain. I remember the date
because it was marked by one particularly traumatic and horribly unfor-
gettable experience, which almost brought everyone's world collapsing in
on top of them – including Philip's.

Shortly before Cathleen was born, in 1980, Thin Lizzy were scheduled
to play a homecoming gig at the RDS Simmonscourt Extension in
Dublin, as part of a massive world tour. It should have been one of those
triumphant emotional occasions which Thin Lizzy's Dublin bashes tended to inspire, and an excited group of family and friends met before the
show at a nearby pub called The Horse Show House, in a decidedly cele-
bratory mood. While the rest of the company prepared to enjoy themselves at a gig which was expected to be as exciting as any of Thin Lizzy's
previous concerts in their home town, I noticed that Caroline seemed to

be out of sorts. Initially, I put that down to her pregnancy, but I became a bit more concerned when she had not improved by the time we went backstage, to the caravan which was normally reserved for close friends of the band.

The gig went ahead, and we all went out to watch, but Caroline clearly wasn't in good shape. Inevitably, when Philip came off the stage at the end of the main part of the show and was preparing for what would have been the first encore, he saw that Caroline was in distress. I presume he was worried that she might be about to go into labour, and I remember him frantically clearing the way for her to get back to the caravan, and ordering someone to call for an ambulance to take her away for medical attention. Meanwhile, outside, the crowd were still demanding an encore, with increasing restlessness.

In the middle of all this, someone in the entourage informed me that Caroline's condition was actually the result of having taken some drugs. Emotions were running high and in the circumstances I probably behaved badly. I remember screaming at Philip that Caroline was not going into labour at all and that he should return to the stage and do his encore for the fans. I really don't know what Philip knew about Caroline's drug use at the time, but I had the impression that he was enraged that, whatever the cause, she had been so careless as to get herself into this kind of predicament during her pregnancy. On the other hand maybe he knew everything, and what we saw was sheer blind anger at the fact that all this was going on in public. Either way, Philip's concern turned to fury and he started angrily lashing out at all the people around him. Back inside the hall, the crowd understandably continued to demand an encore – totally oblivious, naturally, to the intense drama that was taking place backstage. The ambulance was cancelled and Philip himself accompanied Caroline home to Glen Corr.

My own immediate reaction was that Caroline had ruined an important Thin Lizzy gig in Philip's home town, which was in itself inexcusable. Worse still, if she had used drugs while carrying his child, I felt that she could no longer love my son, despite what she might have said herself. Maybe that was a one-sided judgement, especially as I was still unaware that Philip's own entanglement with serious drugs was even more lethal than his wife's.

Worse was to follow. Philip telephoned me later that night at White Horses in Howth, to tell me that Caroline had been taken to hospital in Dublin because he had slapped her. He claimed that she had threatened him with a poker. Naturally, I was horrified at the whole dreadful turn of events, but my first priority was to protect Philip. When I went into the hospital, I was probably close to a nervous breakdown myself. I accused her of ruining a very important night for Philip and of putting his position in jeopardy. I was probably blind to any right which might have been on her side, but she didn't help when she admitted quite openly that she had peed in her clothes to convince Philip her waters had broken. I know that that was just to get out of a violent confrontation, but she really screwed his brain that night, whatever was going on between them.

I was also concerned in case she might tell the doctors that her bruises had resulted from Philip being violent with her. Imagine how that would have looked in the press – a famous, rich rock star beating his pregnant wife after his band's homecoming gig? At the time, that seemed to matter more than anything else, so I reminded her of the things I knew about her and threatened to reveal them all if she did anything to ruin Philip's reputation. I know that this was deplorable behaviour, but the whole situation was out of control, and I wanted to put some kind of brake on it so that at least no further damage could be done.

On the spot, Caroline agreed to stay silent about the incident, although she did later tell some relatives of mine that he had beaten her. I think most people, knowing the truth of their situation, would have understood that any person can only take so much of that sort of behaviour from someone who purports to love him or her. On the other hand, I cannot condone any man, son of mine or not, being violent to a woman at any time, never mind during pregnancy. What he did was wrong and it cannot be justified by reference to the emotional turmoil they were going through.

It wasn't just about drugs either. I don't know how the dates relate but Caroline later confessed to me that her real love was an extremely handsome man who used to work as a lifeguard on the beach near Howth and who was a frequent visitor to Glen Corr. Caroline admitted that she was in love with this man for quite some time, and I believe that their friendship continued after Philip died. I cannot say if they ever actually had an affair. He has personally denied to me that there was ever any sexual relationship between him and Caroline.

Fortunately, Cathleen Elizabeth Lynott was safely born on 29th July 1980, like Sarah, in Holles Street Hospital in Dublin. Shortly after the child's birth, Caroline had another serious bust-up with Philip and I took her into White Horses, where she stayed with me until they both cooled off. There was little I could do to prevent the deterioration of their marriage, particularly when I assumed there must be fault on both sides. In fact, I was conscious that any interference from me might only worsen their difficulties and I was particularly concerned that two young children, innocent bystanders in all this, should be protected from any side-effects of their parents' problems.

It was also important for me to retain Philip's trust and I couldn't do anything to undermine or erode that. By 1980, we had gone into business together. Having missed out on purchasing our first choice, the nearby Royal Howth Hotel, we bought the Asgard Hotel overlooking the bay in Howth for £235,000. We needed to be close to make this venture work, and the domestic havoc wasn't helping in that respect, at all.

The decision to buy the Asgard came about after some typical manipulation on Philip's part. While I was still in Manchester, he called me in a panic about a kitten which he had bought for Sarah – and which had apparently been attacked by a rat. A confirmed animal lover, Philip had even given his publishing company the strange name of Pippin The Friendly Ranger after a kitten. He was concerned that any injury to the kitten might upset little Sarah, so I rushed to Glen Corr only for the kitten to die in my arms. Caroline and I buried its torn body in the garden.

Why I would be needed for such a straightforward domestic incident is hard to explain. In truth, Philip would persuade me to come over to Howth on the most spurious grounds, mainly I think because he wanted me to look after Caroline, who was, after all, living in a strange land away from her own family and personal friends, and was married to a man whose work took him away from the family home for long periods at a stretch. At the very least, it's a recipe for loneliness, and possibly a degree of inevitable heartache. During one such visit, Philip bought me White Horses, another fine house in Howth, and he was obviously convinced that since I had managed a successful hotel in Manchester, I could do likewise in Dublin.

Initially, Graham Cohen and Dennis looked after our affairs in Manchester while I was engrossed in sorting out the arrangements for taking over the Asgard. Eventually we decided to sell the operation in Manchester. We wanted to make our future in Dublin, so Dennis moved over to Howth, and we worked incredibly hard, day and night, and in a fairly short time managed to establish the hotel as a lively business and a popular out-of-town spot for Dubliners. In many ways, I was sad to leave The Clifton Grange Hotel with all its memories, but I was pleased to learn that it was subsequently turned into an old person's home. Maybe I can head back there in a few years!

Whenever he paid a visit to Dublin, no matter how fleeting, Philip spent a good bit of his time at the Asgard, and his regular presence undoubtedly provided a boost for the image of the hotel as we tried to build up its reputation. On one occasion, some guests at a wedding reception spotted him and started making a fuss, so following much persuasion from me, he agreed to dance with the bride. He found such occasions a little demanding and more than a little embarrassing. He often admitted his admiration for Brian Downey's ability, at the end of a tour, to set off on a fishing expedition with his son. He was aware of his own inability to sit and relax for any lengthy period, but Philip had the responsibility of running the band's affairs and that contributed to him burning himself out.

Sometimes, perhaps when he thought everything was going smoothly and he could finally afford to take a break, some fresh problem would arise. Indeed, Thin Lizzy's history is littered with dramatic crises, including Eric Bell's early departure, Brian Robertson's hand injury, Gary Moore's surprise exit during an American tour, Philip's ear problems and the shooting incident – not to mention all the normal personal conflicts that arise when people have to spend so much of their time in close proximity. Philip has been described as an approachable genius who demanded one thousand per cent from everybody in his organisation, including himself, and who would get into a fierce temper if anything went awry. But that kind of intensity, while it may bring success, sometimes also carries a price with it. In fairness to Caroline, I think you have to view all the problems which afflicted their marriage in that light. There are worse fates, I know – but it isn't easy living with a rock star.

When Philip departed on yet one more protracted tour, this time to Australia, Caroline, Sarah and Cathleen continued living in Glen Corr. At the time, Graham Cohen was managing the Asgard and he had agreed to take on the added responsibility of looking after Philip's family when asked to do so by Philip himself – so he moved into the house to keep a watchful eye on things and to provide any back-up that Caroline might need.

Each night, we would finish in the Asgard at about 2.30 a.m. after enjoying our usual drink with the staff. On our way to our own house at White Horses, Dennis and I would lodge the day's takings in the bank's night-safe and drop Graham at Glen Corr.

This routine was followed on numerous occasions without anything untoward happening. So we were more than surprised to arrive at Glen Corr at about 3 a.m. on one particular morning to find all the lights on in the house and rock music blaring out into the night air – a most unusual situation at that time of the morning, especially when we had no knowledge that a party of any kind had been planned. Thinking that perhaps Philip had arrived home unexpectedly, and that a celebration might be in progress, Graham and I ran into the house only to be met by an astonishing sight.

The house was full of kids of both sexes, in their teens, who were drinking, dancing, kissing, partying and lying around everywhere. And there was absolutely no sign of Philip.

My first concern was for Sarah and Cathleen, and I made straight for the nursery where I found Sarah, who was then about four, and Cathleen a year younger, completely unattended. Thankfully, they were sleeping like angels, oblivious to the mayhem going on around them. When I found the door to Philip and Caroline's bedroom ajar, I called out his name, but getting no answer, I pushed it open slightly and went in, as I had done many times before.

Noticing two people in the bed, I went past Caroline, towards two male feet protruding at the other side. Assuming they were Philip's, I started playfully tickling them. But when I pulled the covers back, instead of finding Philip, I discovered a total stranger in bed with my son's wife, who was by now swearing at having been caught red-handed and red-faced in an adulterous situation by her own mother-in-law.

Disgusted and in a raging fury, I rushed from the bedroom past an astonished Graham and towards the kitchen in search of a weapon to use on the man who was occupying my son's marriage bed. I probably would have done something violent if I'd got the chance – and doubtless lived to regret it. Fortunately, Graham wrestled the knife from my hand. Meanwhile, the guy made his escape through the bedroom window and was spotted by Dennis, who had stayed in the car outside the gate waiting for my return, running up the drive struggling to put his trousers on.

When I endeavoured to clear the house of the kids who were partying away, they protested that they could not go home because they had told their parents they were going to an all-night party. Had the situation not been so serious, it would have seemed like a scene from a West End farce.

I spent the next day working at the Asgard and trying to come to terms with the situation. I refused to respond to several attempts by Caroline to reach me by telephone. Her calls continued the following day and, eventually, I reluctantly agreed to meet her – though I really had no idea what was the right thing for me to do in the circumstances. I went to Glen Corr, and when I sat down in an armchair to talk, she sank down on her knees, threw her arms around me and, with her body racked with sobs, begged me not to tell Philip. She kept repeating how much she truly loved him and how sorry she was to have been unfaithful to him.

I asked her how did she think Philip would react if he knew what I had discovered. She said: "He'd kill me." That was what the voice inside my own head had been saying, over and over. I knew that *he'd* take it terribly badly and that he might do something that he'd regret for ever. With that in mind, I told her that I had no intention of reporting her treacherous behaviour to him – because in my eyes she was not worth the possibility that he might end up in prison.

At this, she hugged me and thanked me. With considerable difficulty, and more than a little guilt at the duplicity involved, I managed to avoid telling Philip anything of the incident until much later. But I have asked myself over and over whether telling him the whole story sooner might have brought him abruptly to his senses, and, as a result, altered the course of his life – and who knows, perhaps even his death.

Nor was that an isolated example of strange conduct on Caroline's part while she was living in Glen Corr. One Christmas Eve, I was at White Horses when Philip telephoned me from Glen Corr inviting Dennis and me over for a chat and a Christmas drink. But no sooner had we arrived at the house than Caroline began begging me to accompany her for a Christmas drink in the Cock Tavern, a local pub. When I declined, she persisted, arguing that Philip would let her go if I agreed to go with her. Then when one of our neighbours arrived, and Caroline redoubled her efforts – I finally asked Philip if he would have any objection to Caroline, her friend and I going out for a drink. Philip said he did not mind, as he could then have a chat with Dennis and amuse the children.

In the crowded pub, Caroline bought me a drink and I relaxed, listening to the buzz of conversation and the strains of 'Silent Night'. My son was home for Christmas, delighted to be reunited with his children, and my own relationship with Dennis was going very nicely. I suppose I was feeling content in the way that a nice Christmas Eve can induce. After a while, however, I began to notice that Caroline and her friend had gone missing. When they returned, after what was a long and frustrating wait, they told me that they had visited some other pubs and I assumed they were searching for somebody. After one final drink, I persuaded Caroline, who had driven us there in a Saab Turbo that Philip had recently bought for her, to take me back to Dennis and Philip. But, as we approached the turn across the railway line towards Glen Corr, I was alarmed to find Caroline driving on past the turning and heading further away from the house towards town. They answered my protests by convincing me that they were not going very far, and they would get me home shortly.

Caroline then drove us to a north Dublin suburb called Bayside, where she abruptly stopped the car. She left the radio playing while she and her friend went off, leaving me alone and bewildered in a strange neighbourhood, full of people streaming home after their night's entertainment and last-minute Christmas shopping.

I struggled frantically to get out of the back seat of the two-door car and eventually managed it, hurrying off in the direction of the flats towards which I had seen them go.

I was completely at a loss to know what was going on, and why I was being treated in such a horrible, contemptuous way. I was worried sick, but also in a furious temper. I began calling out for the pair of them at each door in turn, no doubt scaring the wits out of the occupants at the same time, until I finally heard Caroline and her friend running back to the car.

When I demanded of Caroline that she should tell me what the hell was going on, I discovered she had gone to the house of the same man (a drug dealer whose name is known to me and who has since fled from Ireland to Belgium) with whom I had found her in bed months previously. Presumably she wanted something urgently from him, though I never found out what the real purpose of the visit was. When we arrived back outside Glen Corr, she again pleaded with me not to tell Philip.

Inside the house, I found him, the picture of happiness, there with his daughters, chatting contentedly with Dennis and enjoying a drink in front of a big cosy fire while a glowing Christmas tree lit up the room, totally oblivious to what his wife had been up to behind his back. The contradiction between her subterfuge and his innocent happiness brought tears of anger and sadness to my eyes, and I had to retire quickly to the bathroom to compose myself – but I said nothing, rather than risk ruining Christmas for Philip and in particular for the children.

On another occasion, while Philip was away, the unexpected appearance of a young baby and a Rottweiler pup in Glen Corr gave me further reason to wonder what exactly was going on in Caroline's head. I pointed out to her that the pup might be dangerous to have around young children, and besides, that the baby's non-stop screaming was upsetting her own children. She told me that the baby and the dog belonged to a woman who was "an initiated witch" and who had gone to Spain, leaving them in her care.

I thought this was preposterous and I ordered her to pack both baby and dog into her car and to find someone else to mind them. That might make me sound like an awful harridan, but I sensed that there was something extremely odd about the situation. Caroline gave me the impression that the witch had some kind of strange hold over her, although I failed to persuade her to tell me what that might have been. I still don't know the full truth behind that bizarre relationship.

On another occasion, a two-seater couch which had been purchased as part of the furniture with the house disappeared quite suddenly, and Caroline said she had given it to the witch. My own reaction was to won-

SUITABLY ATTIRED: A young Philip all dressed up for the camera.

MERRY PRANKSTER: Philip on his fifth birthday

MAMA'S BOY: Philip with his mother, Philomena, grandmother Sarah and Brian Downey.

Pic: Roy Esmonde

DAPPER DAN: A youthful Philip cuts a dash

BALLAD OF A THIN MAN: Early Decca publicity shot – so early, in fact, that the record company's own caption reads "Tim Lizzy".

COOL CAT: Philip pictured for an interview to promote the *Renegade* album.

WEDDING DAY: Caroline, Philip and Sarah.

AND THEN THERE WERE FOUR: Gary Moore enters the picture

PHIL LYNOTT (Thin Lizzy)

HOT UNDER THE COLLAR: Philip dons clerical garb.

GOT MY CYCLE OUTSIDE: Philip motorbikin'.

GUITAR MAN: Philip swapping lead and bass.

ON THE BOARDS: Echoes of Hendrix as Philip strikes a classic pose.

LIVE AND DANGEROUS: Philip caught in the act

PHILIP PARRIS LYNOTT

1949 ~ 1986

Go dtuga Dia
suaimhneas da anam

Róisín Dubh

FINAL
RESTIN
PLACE:
The Jim
Fitzpatric
designed
headstone
Philip's
grave in
Sutton, C
Dublin.

der what else might have been given away to this woman, who obviously had some mysterious grip on Caroline.

All of these events made me ponder what state their marriage was in, but I also knew that marriages can overcome the most extraordinary difficulties. While things were clearly awry, there was no reason to think that a breakdown was inevitable, if both people involved resolved to behave maturely and lovingly. But I cannot claim that Philip himself was any more capable of knowing what that meant than Caroline at that time. It would be hypocritical to pretend that he was incapable of similar infidelities, and I was not naive enough to believe that Philip would ignore the endless stream of young women who inexplicably make themselves available to celebrities. But at no stage was I aware of any serious extra-marital relationship he might have enjoyed.

I suppose that's the difference when someone is on the road – at least they're unlikely to become involved in binding relationships. There were, however, many times when I called to the house in Kew to find some young attractive girl staying there under unusual circumstances. If I enquired about her presence, I would be informed that she was a friend of someone else. Even if I suspected he was lying to me, I probably accepted it as the way of the world in those changing times. But I didn't like it.

If personal relationships in the small family were beginning to fragment, so too were business arrangements. Not that there was anything that could have been done to prevent this particular calamity. The Asgard Hotel was burned down in the early hours of an August Bank Holiday morning, in 1982. At almost that precise moment, Philip was arriving back at Glen Corr from a tour. The blaze happened only about eight months after we had bought the Asgard, just as the business was beginning to thrive. Firemen fighting the flames were hampered by a loss of water pressure because of a simultaneous gorse fire on nearby Howth Head, and there was nothing they could do to prevent its virtual annihilation.

When we arrived at the blazing building, Philip put his arm around me and said, "Never mind, Ma, I'll buy you another one!" But the truth is that we both lost a lot of money on account of that fire. Bono of U2 has since told me that his father Bobby currently lives in the block of flats they built on the site. It's strange how things so often come full circle in a small city like Dublin that in many ways has the character of a village.

When all is said and done, I have to say that it came as no great shock to me when Philip telephoned from London to tell me that Caroline had left him and taken the kids with her to a house in Corston, near her parents' home in Bath. He then persuaded me to move into Glen Corr – he was obviously worried about his dog, Gnasher, named after Dennis The Menace's dog in *The Beano*, a very popular weekly comic for children – "children of all ages", I suppose – in the 1960s and 70s. Having moved into Glen Corr myself, I rented out White Horses.

When I heard that Caroline was seeking a separation on the grounds of his alleged adultery, I blew my top. At that stage, I had no option but to tell Philip about the night I discovered her in his bed, in his own house, with another man, and he nearly collapsed. I had to apologise for keeping that incident and others from him. Whatever else Philip thought of her and any affairs he might have suspected her of having, surely he never could have imagined that his own mother would find his wife in his house and in his bed with another man. But I suppose he had his own ghosts that were better left undisturbed, and from everyone's point of view, it was best not to become embroiled in a bitter courtroom battle.

The hearing was a quiet event and, in due course, a court order was issued stipulating that Sarah and Cathleen could spend time with Philip, provided I was present at all times during their visits. Caroline knew I loved them and that the children and I got on very well together. As a result, I flew over nearly every fortnight to London to see the girls, and to be present when Caroline brought them to meet Philip.

There were no overt signs of any drug-related health problems in his life, although I now know that Caroline was aware of the full extent of Philip's drug problem. Maybe that was the real reason for the separation, because if there's one thing that someone who is attempting to come to terms with a drug problem *doesn't* need, it's someone who's still using and flaunting the stuff in front of them. I would imagine that that was at least an element in Caroline's decision to leave him.

The girls generally stayed with Caroline in her own house in Bath during this time, and despite the break-up, she remained on cordial terms with both Philip and me. In fact, they were on friendlier terms now than in the period immediately prior to the split, a situation that was doubtlessly influenced by Caroline's positive efforts at cleaning up her own drug problem.

Most times, she would drop the girls off at the Kew house, but I often went in a chauffeur-driven car to Bath to collect them.

Philip worshipped his two girls and not having easy access to them was a big wrench for him. He would try not to miss being in Dublin for Saint Patrick's Day or Easter, and he would fly over with the girls to stay with me for those important occasions, but always with Caroline's approval. As far as I could ascertain, Caroline was always happy to have me there with Philip and the girls, because she was to one degree or another pre-occupied with her own personal problems at the time. She knew he loved them and she knew I would make a fuss of them and that they would return home to her in a very happy mood. That arrangement continued for the remaining years of his life, with me always present at their get-togethers, whether in Glen Corr or in Kew.

Philip and Caroline often referred to their break-up as a trial separation, and she would sometimes spend the week with her mother and stay with Philip at weekends. I often found them in Kew sitting together on a settee with her head in his lap, so there were obviously times when they might have made a real attempt to rescue the marriage. I was often confused by their contradictory behaviour and, in a strange way, it is of some consolation to me that they never actually divorced, a step which has such dreadful finality about it.

Now that I can look back objectively, I think Caroline may have been trying to encourage him to come off the drugs, but with so many creeps hanging around him, and his own constant denials, that was virtually impossible. He never got the space to clean up which she created for herself, I have to be honest, by leaving him. In fairness, too, it would probably not have been practical for them to resume their marriage relationship while he was still using drugs and she was battling to get off them, especially with the two girls to consider. So, much as I loved Philip, and initially felt angry at the way in which she left him, in the end you have to recognise that it was probably the right decision – for her, at least.

On arriving at Kew, you rang a bell beside the large electric gates. One day, having dropped by unexpectedly, I spotted a blonde girl on the premises. Yet again, Philip told me that she was with one of the other chaps. Of course, by this stage I was too disillusioned to be taken in. I assumed that Philip had normal, healthy, male sexual appetites, but he would generally try to prevent me from knowing about specific relationships and therefore I had no real notion as to how he satisfied his carnal urges. I figured this one fell into that category, and no mistake. Had he still been married, I would almost certainly have given him an earful over it, but his marriage was to all intents and purposes over, and he was a free man in my eyes.

It was still a pretty uncomfortable situation. While I was in his bedroom updating him on the news from Dublin, we caught this dreadful, greasy smell from the kitchen where the girl was attempting to cook Philip's breakfast. The smell was so bad that I had to go out into the back garden for some fresh air. She was undaunted and, despite the smell, took this dreadful mess of food up to him. I don't know about him, but I'd have gagged on it. When I again asked who this young woman was, he just grinned sheepishly, and I got the picture. So there is no question in my mind that he was quite capable of lying to me during that period, particularly if he was embarrassed about something.

That house in Kew was a lovely place and I loved staying there. It was situated on about half an acre of land close to the famous Kew Botanical Gardens, and it was worth about £250,000 even at that time. While in retrospect, it is obvious that Philip was spending a lot of money on hard drugs, it never affected the pleasant atmosphere of the house – nor did it seem to create any financial problems for him. I had never quizzed him about his financial or property dealings anyway. But when he became famous first, he loved being able to give us all a good time. From 1976, when the *Jailbreak* album was a huge hit – it went on to sell nearly two million copies – and 'The Boys Are Back In Town' hit the top 20 on both sides of the Atlantic, Thin Lizzy had generated a lot of money.

When the band split up, the gravy train might have stopped rolling, and Philip was certainly hurt and frustrated by the fact that he couldn't get a deal for Grand Slam, the band he attempted to launch in the 80s. At the same time, his solo career had already seen him enjoy hit singles with 'Yellow Pearl', which was used for a long time as the signature tune of the BBC television programme *Top Of The Pops*, and 'King's Call', his tribute to the great Elvis Presley. There were even constant rumours of an imminent and potentially lucrative Thin Lizzy re-union for both an album and a world tour – in fact when you think about it, they could probably have re-grouped to go on to even greater things after a protracted sabbatical, if more momentous events hadn't taken over.

Since the band had enjoyed over a dozen hits in the British album charts and over twenty hit singles in Britain, apart from the others successes elsewhere around the world, many observers may have assumed that there was a bottomless pit of money, but the Thin Lizzy operation had been expensive. The uninitiated tend to overlook the fact that offices, staff and countless other expenses have to be paid for, and the money has to come from somewhere. But it was the general belief among those who knew him, myself included, that he still had a plentiful supply of money, and that he could easily afford to continue the lifestyle to which he had become accustomed – and perhaps, in time, find another woman with whom to build a permanent relationship and a happy home life. As far as I was concerned, he was still a young man with lots to give to the world and – potentially, at least – a long, rewarding life ahead of him.

Christmas has always been one of my favourite times of year. When you have been as poor as I had been in the early years of my life, there is an added quality to the pleasures and indulgences of the festive season, once you're in a position to enjoy them. I love everything about Christmas: the food, the songs, the reunions, the decorations and, most of all, the glowing, expectant faces of children as they unwrap their presents.

Christmas 1985 should have been among the happiest of my life. Certainly, in the weeks leading up to it, I was as excited as a little girl, busily buying gifts for everybody and making plans for the holiday revelry. Little did I know then that I was only days away from the worst nightmare imaginable.

After their separation, Philip and Caroline had agreed that they would spend every Christmas together with the girls. But with less than a fortnight to go before Christmas 1985, Philip's last Christmas on earth, Caroline telephoned me to say that she would prefer not to join us this year in Kew. She asked me to persuade Philip and the two girls to come to Dublin to stay in Glen Corr instead.

I explained that Philip had already decided only to spend the New Year in Dublin, and that he was unlikely to be talked into a change of plan. I agreed to try to bring him round if I could, but it was to no avail, so I flew to London about a week before Christmas, knowing that Caroline would not be joining us. I knew that it would be a somewhat less festive occasion for everyone as a result – but there was no option but to get on with it. Or at least that's what I thought.

When I arrived at the Kew house, I was impressed by the sight, through the front window, of a beautifully-lit Christmas tree and a life-size cardboard promotional cut-out of Philip standing beside it. Philip was in his underpants when he opened the door to greet me. It was now mid-afternoon and he apologised for the fact that he hadn't got dressed yet. I followed him upstairs as he returned to his bed. We discussed a few minor matters and he told me that Big Charlie, as we always called Charlie McLennan, who was one of Philip's most trusted and loyal minders, would be joining us for the holiday, because he had recently split with the woman he had lived with for several years. He also asked me to collect Sarah and Cathleen in Bath.

I was struck immediately by how untidy his room was, cluttered with a mess of take-away food packages, empty bottles and general litter. Worse, Philip looked and sounded decidedly unhealthy, with his excessive weight, cloudy eyes, clogged nasal passages, and the sigh and rasp of his breathing. God, I know now that I should have sensed just how bad his physical condition was but you always want to believe that everything will be OK, and I did.

When I asked why he was in bed so late in the day, he blamed a hang-over from the office party the night before. I accepted this explanation, and assumed that it also warranted his sickly appearance. But he bright-ened up considerably when he showed me a box of small toys he had bought to put in the girls' Christmas stockings. In what was a remarkable and, in retrospect, moving reversion to his childhood, we amused our-selves for a time playing with them on the floor.

When I asked him what would he like from me for his main Christmas present, apart from the customary shirt and underpants, he described an elaborate tree-like lamp he had spotted somewhere. He pointed to a place in the room where he thought it would fit perfectly, but when he told me it would cost £330, I laughed and told him I was not paying that for a lamp. I said I would spend up to £30. He said, "OK, you're on," and we laughed heartily at the whole idea of it, in the way we often did in each other's company.

Later, I went on a shopping expedition into nearby Richmond, during which I purchased some spectacles with tinted lenses for myself. When I came back, Philip announced that the spectacles would be his present for me and, although he passed away before he could reimburse me for them, I will always treasure them as his last gift to me.

On answering a ring at the door, I found a man with two large boxes, which I signed for. One of them contained a lamp which turned out to be exactly the type that Philip had talked me into getting him for Christmas. We laughed again about the way he had wound me up. He then showed me some beautiful wrapping paper featuring Marilyn Monroe, and asked me to help him to wrap his presents for him. Not long afterwards, Jimmy Bain, from the British heavy rock band Rainbow, who was a close friend of Brian Robertson, arrived to stay over. He had apparently separated from his wife, Lady Sophie, daughter of the Marquis of Bute. Philip really liked their daughter, Samantha, who was a perfect playmate for Sarah and Cathleen, and so they had become buddies. Jimmy was eager to show off his new overcoat and knee-high boots, which I figured were part of an obvious attempt to dress like Philip, but because he was small they frankly looked ridiculous on him. Out of politeness, and not wishing to deflate his pleasure at his new purchases, I refrained from anything but encouraging comment.

I immediately regretted that I had not told him precisely what I thought of his ludicrous get-up. Philip called down the stairs for him to come up and Bain said to me with real vehemence: "He thinks I'm his fucking butler." I was staggered at the idea of a man who was about to enjoy another man's generous hospitality over the Christmas period coming out with such language in front of his host's mother. I left the room in disgust, but it brought to mind a recent warning from my brother Peter.

Having visited London and called Philip, he told me that I ought to do something about the situation because there was something strange going on at the Kew house. "There's something wrong with Philip. He's not right and I don't like it," had been his very words, but I discovered too late that they had carried more significance than I imagined. The awful truth is that that was the only hint I ever had from anyone else that Philip's lifestyle had become a real worry. Many of his so-called friends knew the situation was serious, yet they all kept it quiet, and in that sense I think some of them at least can be accused of complicity in his death.

I left to collect the girls in Bath. I don't know who had screwed up on arrangements, but when I got there Caroline told me that they had both been given parts in a nativity play in the local church hall. I agreed to stop overnight with them and enjoyed a very pleasant night, watching my grandchildren innocently perform in a nice play in front of an audience that included both their grannies, their grandfather Leslie, and Caroline. In retrospect, it was like another world.

Arriving back at the Kew house on the following day, the girls were immediately disappointed to notice the Christmas tree wasn't lit, and I thought that it was odd. It turned out to be a bizarre omen. When Philip answered the door in his dressing gown, I again thought this was weird, but I dismissed my concern on the basis that a lot of Philip's work was done at night, at gigs or in the studio, and that his lifestyle was utterly different from mine. Showbiz people are generally night people – or that was how I subliminally rationalised the situation.

I was even further perturbed, however, to discover the offensive Jimmy Bain wrapping his own presents using Philip's nice Marilyn Monroe paper. It was only a small thing, but it got to me. "What a cheap bastard you are," I thought to myself. "You accept a man's hospitality, make insulting remarks about him in front of his mother and you could not even buy your own wrapping paper." That disgusted me so much I could not bring myself to speak to him, and so I avoided communicating with him from then on, except for the occasional dirty look.

Meanwhile, Philip and the girls were sitting on his bed watching a video he had purchased especially for them and they had great fun together. But still, I was becoming increasingly concerned by the fact that

Philip showed few signs of even bothering to get up.

On my suggestion, he arranged for us to go to The Barbican to see a pantomime starring Sting's Irish ex-wife, Frances Tomelty, whom I knew from a film she had shot at The Biz during my Manchester days.

We were joined by a son of Rolling Stone Ron Wood – apparently Philip had got to know the boy very well, because his mother was friendly with Brian Robertson.

The following day, Philip was still unable to get up. He told me that he was expecting a man to call, and asked me to give the caller a cheque which he had hidden under a garden gnome outside the front door. This was so suspicious, that I must admit I suspected it might be payment for a consignment of drugs. When the man called, I recognised him immediately as a certain unsavoury Mr. Kelly, who had been involved with Philip before.

I asked him straight out if he worked for Philip, and when he didn't answer I tore up the cheque in anger right before his eyes and threatened to telephone the police as he ran off in fright. But not even that incident had brought home to me the depths to which my son had sunk in his drug addiction.

While I was downstairs taking a telephone message, I suddenly noticed water dripping from the ceiling. Assuming there must be a pipe leaking, I dashed upstairs. To my absolute horror, I found Philip fully clothed, wearing his jumper and jacket, floating in the bath while water splashed out over the sides. "What on earth do you think you're doing?" I asked him, as I pulled out the plug. But he just kept trying to pour hot water on himself, all the time crying out, "Ma, I'm freezing. I'm freezing. I can't get warm."

I was terrified. There was no-one else anywhere to be seen – and how was I, a late middle-aged woman, looking after two children, to get him, a big man made even heavier with the weight of his wet clothes, out of the bath? Somehow, however, I found superhuman strength and managed to get him back to his bed. After drying him off, I tucked him in, as warm as

I could. I had no idea what else to do.

It is so hard thinking about all this, remembering it, writing about it. I was confused and I have to admit that I probably made the wrong decisions. If I had called an ambulance and had him taken to hospital, it's possible that Philip might have lived but I really had no idea of the extent to which he was physically ravaged by the drugs he had been taking.

On Christmas Eve, I took the girls into his room for a goodnight Christmas kiss from their Dad. When they returned to their own room after the usual kidding around, he called them back and hugged them both again. I can only think now that there was some kind of sixth sense at work, because a short time later he began vomiting. When I asked him what did he think was wrong, he looked at me helplessly, tears of embarrassment and pity welling up in his eyes, and said, "Ma, I don't know."

By now, my anxiety had become so intense that I telephoned Dennis in Ireland and told him what was happening. We agreed that Graham would fly over to join me, while Dennis would stay on to look after Glen Corr. Meanwhile, I decided that further delay might be dangerous, so I called a local doctor whose name I had found in the telephone directory. In due course, he arrived and wrote a prescription which I immediately took to the nearest chemist. At that point, I think the doctor thought he was suffering from gastro-enteritis or some sort of flu. Unfortunately, the medicine which was prescribed only seemed to make him worse.

I keep thinking about ways in which things might have been done differently, and how it might have been possible to save my beautiful boy's life. I imagine, for example, that Philip might have been able to tell the doctor about his drug problem had I not stayed with him in the room. In my distress, I didn't want to leave him – I wanted to hear every word that was being said so that I could nurse him as effectively as possible. Later, I realised that calling that particular doctor was probably a mistake. Not being made aware of any of the details of Philip's drug addiction, he may have assumed he was merely suffering a bilious attack, hardly uncommon around Christmas-time. All day long, after the doctor had left, I trudged up and down to Philip with various kinds of drinks but they mostly remained untouched. There was no sign of any improvement.

Meanwhile, Robbo arrived with some of his friends and I told him how worried I was about Philip's condition, and about the doctor and the fact that the prescription did not seem to have helped Philip at all. Without further comment, Robbo instantly told me I should have called a doctor they knew as "The Quack" or "Doctor Diamond."

Shortly afterwards Graham arrived, and the doctor Robbo recommended also came over. We took the doctor to Philip's room, filling him in about the previous doctor's visit, but to my amazement, instead of tending to my sick son, he simply started casually looking through Philip's collection of video tapes! Maybe he was waiting for a signal because Philip then asked me to leave the room and I joined Robbo downstairs.

Ashen-faced, Robbo explained to me that Philip had a serious drug problem and that this was, almost certainly, at the root of his current malaise. While I was still reeling from the shock of this news, I was informed that the doctor had injected Philip with something. I never have been able to find out precisely what the injection comprised or what effect it was expected to have. On the surface at least, "The Quack" was still behaving quite casually about the whole affair and simply told us to leave Philip for twelve hours, but to call him if his condition deteriorated. He dismissed Philip's problem as simply a dose of flu and, at the time, in my state of numb disbelief, I found his casual attitude rather reassuring, and my worries subsided somewhat.

All through the night, Robbo, Graham and I took turns tending to Philip, and I was heartened to see that at least there seemed to be no worsening in his condition. On Christmas Day, Big Charlie dropped by, and I gladly welcomed him. I told him that Philip had informed me that he would be spending Christmas with us. I remember sitting on the settee, telling Charlie how sick Philip seemed and how confused I felt about the whole situation. Since the doctor had been so casual, I temporarily disregarded Robbo's claim that Philip had a serious drug problem but I now wanted Charlie to tell me the whole truth.

Charlie looked at me in disbelief. "Has nobody told you the full story yet?" he asked. And then he told me the horrible unavoidable truth that I had been hiding from – or that had been hidden from me – all those years.

When he explained that Philip had been using heavy drugs for well over ten years, I was astounded. My son, I was now informed, had a serious heroin problem. But even as the awful truth sank in, I could not have imagined that his condition had deteriorated to the point where he had little more than ten days to live.

After breaking the dreadful news to me, Charlie ran up the stairs and burst into Philip's bedroom. "Philip, I've told Phyllis the truth. She has a right to know," he said.

All the suspicions I had been trying to avoid were crystallised by what Charlie had told me. I was shattered now that I knew what had really been going on. Just then the phone rang. It was 3 o'clock on Christmas Day and Caroline was calling with Christmas greetings. I was in agony and broke down as I tried to tell her about Philip's distressful situation. I told her about the two doctors and what they had done, and she said, "Don't worry, I know exactly what to do. I'll be with you in an hour and a half, and I'll book him into a clinic."

When Charlie arrived back downstairs, I told him about Caroline's call and we were both considerably relieved. I don't know about anyone else who was there, but I really had no idea how physically broken he was by the drugs, and I was searching for light – any kind of light – at the end of what only part of me would concede was a tunnel of nightmarish darkness.

I simply wanted all this talk of heroin and sickness to stop, and for Philip to return to his old invincible self. We began to pack his bag for the hospital trip, re-assured with the knowledge that he would shortly be in the hands of professional people who I, at least, imagined would soon have him on the mend.

THE FINAL DYING OF THE LIGHT

"Death is no easy answer
For those who wish to know
Ask those who have been before you
What fate the future holds."
– from 'Warriors' by Philip Lynott

Caroline arrived and explained precisely how to get to the Clouds Clinic in East Knoyle, near Salisbury in Wiltshire. She had already arranged for Philip to be admitted immediately on his arrival. She then took the two girls, Sarah and Cathleen, with her to her own place in Bath, while Big Charlie and Graham Cohen drove Philip in a separate car to the Clouds Clinic. Though sick with worry, I remained behind to take care of the house, and I waited there for news, for what seemed like an eternity.

My anxiety was further exacerbated when Charlie and Graham arrived back from Wiltshire, late on Christmas night, with the bad news that Philip had only spent about forty minutes in Clouds, where he had not responded to treatment. A Dr. McCann at the clinic had advised that Philip, now almost in a coma, should be taken directly to Salisbury General Infirmary.

In retrospect, of course, it would have been better had Philip been taken from the house in Kew to the nearest emergency hospital, rather than being driven 180 miles to Clouds, but it is easy to be clever when you know these things in hindsight. At the time it seemed like the right decision. That's all I can say now.

Graham had accompanied Philip in the ambulance, with Charlie travelling separately behind, on the hour-long journey to the Infirmary, where Philip was admitted to the emergency unit on arrival. At least, I thought, I could finally take some comfort from knowing that he was, at last, receiving proper medical treatment. The doctors, I kept telling myself, would do whatever was necessary to restore my son to health as soon as possible. Even at that stage, I wasn't remotely considering the possibility of my boy's death.

Charlie and Graham promised to take me to the Infirmary later in the day to visit Philip. At about six o'clock on the morning of St Stephen's Day (Boxing Day in Britain), I was awoken from a fitful, delirious sleep by an apparition at the foot of my bed telling me that a policeman had called to say that Philip was still not responding to treatment. Such was the impact of this latest bulletin of bad news that I did not realise that the "apparition" was actually Graham. But the implication of the message was impossible to ignore. Nausea and panic began to take hold. I desperately wanted to be with him.

I can remember little of the bleak journey to Salisbury which I began at six o'clock on a cold winter's morning. Nor did I realise that I would be with my son virtually every moment for the rest of his life. I would not leave the vicinity of the hospital for eleven excruciating, lonely, brutal, heartbreaking days.

Philip had been given a room of his own and was propped up in bed when I first saw him. A nurse was busy taking blood samples from his arm. I was delighted to find that he was conscious. I said, "Hello, love," and he weakly said, "I'm all right, Ma." We talked for a while, but he kept nodding off and I assumed that he was drowsy from whatever medication they might have given him. I, too, was weary from the trauma of it all and I would doze off intermittently.

I have one very fond memory of those first few hours. While I was sitting in an armchair with my feet up on his bed. I asked Philip for a smile and he grinned sheepishly at me.

Inevitably, word of his hospitalisation had leaked out. When requests came from friends and fans wishing to visit him, I decided that receiving visitors would be too much of a strain for him. I had to insist that no-one would be allowed in to see him, except immediate friends or family. I wanted to give him every opportunity to recover without any energy-draining distractions – although, at this stage, nobody at the hospital had told me anything about his actual condition, or how critical it might be.

Now that he was in the intensive care unit, I was totally convinced that he would recover before too long, and I would not risk any unnecessary intrusion that might hinder that process. He had no visitors at all during the first four days, apart from Caroline, Charlie, Graham and myself. Other than Graham, who stayed with me all the time, and Big Charlie, who made daily visits, very few people were allowed to go near him during his hospitalisation. We kept the children away until later. Caroline's sister Charlotte, his manager Chris Morrison and his agent John Salter, came and brought a chap called Paul Mauger who was already known to be a big fan of Philip's and has since been acknowledged as the leading expert on Philip's recording and performing career. But I don't remember anyone else being admitted and it was probably just as well.

I was struck by the fact that no members of the band came, although in fairness, they may not have known the full extent of his illness because it was Christmas-time and news took longer than usual to get through. Lots of fans called, but I had to be resolute and explain that any exertion might hinder Philip's recovery. I promised they could all visit him when he was restored to his full health, but now certainly wasn't the time to pay their respects.

Christmas also meant that the hospital was short-staffed and, over the following days, I helped with a lot of basic chores myself, including washing him, cleaning his teeth, getting him to spit out and so on. Graham, who was wonderfully loyal and a source of strength throughout, would wash Philip's body for me every single day.

There has since been much offensive and ill-founded conjecture about Philip's body being covered in open sores and marks during his final days.

I can completely refute those rumours, as can Graham. The worst that could be said about his overall physical condition was that he was overweight. However, there was one utterly unexpected detail that thoroughly shocked me. I was truly staggered when I saw the state of the toes of both feet, where Philip had obviously been injecting himself. For the briefest of moments, I thought the navy blue colour of his feet was merely the result of the cold and chills, but the horrible graphic truth of the extent of his addiction was finally beginning to sink home.

Some people may, I know, object to my going into the unpleasant details of Philip's death so thoroughly. But there are two main reasons for me doing so. First, there has been much inaccurate speculation in the media about the circumstances of his death and, since I was there through every minute of his final days, I think it is important to put the real facts on the record once and for all, to avoid any further distortion of the truth. Perhaps more importantly, I would like everybody out there, particularly young people, to know that heroin addiction really does lead to a gruesome and very undignified, unpleasant end. If Philip's death can have any value, maybe a full understanding of this harsh reality might stop others following down that miserable, hellish path.

And make no mistake – these are not the words of some do-gooder who is simply out to deny people the right to live their life to the full. This is the woebegone testimony of a woman who has been there, seen that and done everything she could to help her son recover – to no avail. I have often thought since of the irony in the fact that Philip's unexpected conception had cut short my studies to enter the nursing profession – and now, here I was, nursing him as his life slowly ebbed away.

All day, I would remain by his bedside. Then, at night, I would usually retire to a bungalow in the grounds, where the hospital had arranged some sleeping accommodation for me. After a few days, Graham kindly agreed to travel back to Kew to get me a badly-needed change of clothes – I realised with some embarrassment that I had been wearing the same items since arriving at the hospital.

That Philip was very sick could not now be in doubt. I realised that he had not urinated at all, since I had arrived at the hospital. When I brought this to the attention of a nurse, it immediately resulted in pandemonium, because a failure to urinate could be an indication that his kidneys were not functioning properly. He was rapidly placed on a dialysis machine, which seemed to restore some function to his kidneys. However, he had by now developed symptoms of pneumonia, and so also had to be attached to a respirator. The odds were beginning to stack up against him.

In intensive care, Philip shared a room with two other patients. One had suffered a heart attack and he told me his son worked on the royal yacht Britannia. The other patient was a wee baby, about a year old, whose parents had been told me might be suffering from a brain defect. The sight of his frail body took me right back to the turmoil of my son's early days, while the same Philip fought for his life in another bed.

The long and lonely wait was excruciating but at least there were some creature comforts to alleviate the stress marginally. The unit was adjacent to a very pleasant room, equipped with a television and coffee-making equipment for which you could buy coffee in the hospital shop. I spent some time in that room with the distraught relatives of the other two patients. In my desire to be strong for them, I convinced myself that Philip was bound to recover.

During one of my brief interludes in that rest room, I was interrupted by a young girl who sought me out in the room and handed me a bunch of flowers. But whatever it was about her manner, I quickly realised that she was a reporter. I refused to talk to her and she eventually departed. Little did I realise then that for the rest of my life I would have to cope with the intrusions of the media, a few of whom would stoop to any level, tell any lie or use any despicable trick to get their stories – which, more often than not, are transformed into a mixture of fact and fantasy anyway.

When Caroline told me that she was bringing the two girls to see their father in hospital, I tried to dissuade her on the grounds that Philip was connected to several tubes, and seeing him in this condition might not be right for the children. But she believed they should see each other, and I accept that she was probably right. When Philip saw the two girls through the glass, he did not have the strength to do anything more than cry – the tears rolled down his cheeks. Who knows what thoughts were going through his head at this time? Did he realise that he would never again see the two daughters he loved with all his heart?

By the time New Year's Eve arrived, TV cameras were virtually camped outside the hospital gates, and fans were sleeping rough and hoping to be allowed in. I was feeling tired and unkempt and I needed a change of clothes. Graham found a way for me to escape undetected and took me to a convenient branch of Marks And Spencers. I did some other shopping, but I was locked into the nightmare that was unwinding remorselessly at the hospital, and I can remember physically shaking with worry for Philip as I moved around the shops like a zombie.

My mood was in sharp contrast to the carol singing and general air of festivity common to Christmas-time, and nowhere more so than in the beautiful, quaint cathedral town of Salisbury where my son would breathe his last. Beautiful music, including a favourite song of mine by Paul Robeson, poured from loudspeakers around the centre of the town, and I could see so many happy faces. But my heart was like lead, and there was a dreamlike quality to my grim detachment from the prevailing atmosphere of good humour and merriment.

At the hospital, it was difficult for me to get any clear indication regarding Philip's condition. This may have been because the staff were uncertain about whom to give priority to – to me as his mother, or to Caroline, who, although they had been estranged, was still his wife. An encounter with Caroline in the hospital corridor did little to relieve my gloom. "Do you realise that there is a real possibility that Philip could die?" she said to me. For the first time, I think, I gathered that the hospital staff felt that he might not pull through and I presumed that they had communicated this reality to her.

To clear up another malicious story that has been told and retold, there is absolutely no truth whatsoever in the suggestion that Caroline had callously let Philip suffer for days at home before getting him to hospital. I know because I was there and, here again, I think it is important that the truth be told. Right from the moment that she knew there was a serious problem, she did what she believed to be best for Philip. Any other suggestion is simply a distortion or a lie – or both.

My gradual comprehension that his death was a genuine possibility made it even more difficult for me the next time I went to bathe Philip's face as I had regularly been doing. I was anxious not to allow him to see any fear in my eyes, because I believe a sick person can see that fear and it only adds to their own difficulties. So I put on my most cheerful disposition, and told him not to worry, that as soon as he was on the mend I would take him back with me to Ireland and get him right again. But inside, the emotional turmoil was killing me.

It was then that he spoke these very words to me. "Merciful Jesus, what have I done to you, Ma?" he said, in his own inimitable Dublin accent. I can still see the forlorn look in his eyes and I have carried his trembling voice, the voice of a drowning man, as it echoes those words in my head to this day. It was horrifying, truly horrifying, to sit there and know that there was no way back. I tried to put on my bravest face and kept repeating: "Don't worry, I'll get you better." However, I think that was the precise moment when both he and I faced the reality of his imminent death.

When I left the room, I met a man of the cloth in the corridor, and I heard him asking a nurse for directions to Philip Lynott's room. Almost hysterically, I pleaded with him not to go into the room with his collar on, for fear it might frighten Philip, but he calmly interrupted my pleas to tell me that Philip had asked for him. I just stood aside and let him pass and then rushed to the bathroom in great distress.

There was a terrible sense of impending doom in Philip's apparent resignation. I felt sick with anxiety and fear.

At midnight, the hospital and the surrounding town reverberated with the New Year celebrations. The nurses on duty popped open champagne bottles and I did what I could to join in the festivities. It was a desperate sham, but I took some bubbly in to Philip and, wishing him a Happy New Year, I allowed three or four drops to fall onto his tongue. My heart almost burst with joy when he smiled at me, smacked his lips at the taste of the champagne and mischievously asked for more. Laughing, I told him to behave himself and, after one more sip, we sang 'Auld Lang Syne' together.

Shortly after midnight, I spoke to the doctor in charge and he gave me the good news that Philip's kidneys had started to function again. Despite the roller-coaster emotions of the previous day, I went to my room in the little bungalow with a lighter heart and a renewed sense of optimism. Maybe everything was going to be all right after all.

Over the following days I remained optimistic. Without any word to the contrary, I convinced myself that it was simply a matter of time before Philip would begin to recover. I imagined, over and over again, the moment when he would be discharged – and life would begin to return to normal again.

My fragile elation continued until the night of 3rd January. To this day, I am convinced that Graham and Big Charlie knew how grave the situation was that night but, for my own protection, they colluded to get me away from the hospital by escorting me back to the house in Kew, with the reassurance that they would send for me immediately if there were any developments. In fairness, I think it was better for me, and possibly for Philip as well, that I was not around when the situation began to seriously deteriorate.

Back at the house, there was a continuous barrage of phone-calls from the media and from friends, all enquiring after Philip. My niece, Monica, volunteered to deal with the torrent of queries and good wishes. However, I was terrified that she would get some important news and not pass it on to me immediately, so I persuaded her to follow a procedure of answering each call then telling me instantly who the caller was.

Then the call that I had been dreading came through.

Philip was dead.

The news sliced through me, from head to toe, like a scalpel-sharp blade. No matter that I had an inkling that he had been close to death's door – now that it had happened, I couldn't believe it. In my hysteria, I ran outside and tried to get through the main gates, an impossible task since they were electrically-operated from inside the house. I was going demented, screaming and roaring for my son. When Caroline arrived from the hospital and told me again, in person, I could no longer control myself. I sank to my knees and started banging my head against the ground in utter, inconsolable grief.

My only son, with whom I had experienced so many trials and tribulations and shared the joys and sorrows of life, was dead at the appallingly young age of 36. His ravaged body gave up the struggle on Saturday 4th January 1986, leaving two daughters, aged eight and five, a widow of twenty-seven, and a heartbroken mother behind to grieve for him.

"They buried my body and they thought I'd gone
But I am the dance and I still live on."
– from 'Lord Of The Dance' by Sidney Carter

The period immediately following the devastating news of Philip's death is still lost for me in a haze of agony and deep distress. I can remember only some of the events that were taking place all around me. Graham came to Kew to take me back to Salisbury to identify Philip's body. But I was so distraught, I could not bring myself to do it. He and Caroline bravely carried out that gruesome duty instead.

At some point, I was shown a brochure and asked to select a coffin but I could not bear to look at the photographs. Again, Graham and Caroline chose the casket in which Philip was buried. I'm not sure that it was the most appropriate response at all because I was clearly in a state of denial. Not only did I never see his body in death, but I even forced myself, by clenching my eyes shut if necessary, not to look at the casket either. This may have been the only way I could have dealt with his death, by refusing to acknowledge that it had happened at all. But there is a price to pay because you can't keep running away from reality, no matter how grim, forever.

On returning from the hospital, Graham handed me an envelope containing the jewellery which Philip had been wearing when he died, as well as a lock of his hair which I still have in my possession. Then, Caroline wanted to know if I felt he should be buried wearing his wedding ring and I said no. These are the crazy issues people feel that they have to concern themselves with when somebody dies – especially someone who is young. However trivial it may seem now, I made that decision because he was not married when he died, not because of any anger with Caroline. I have never believed in the custom of burying people with jewellery anyway.

The hospital's pathologist, Dr. Angela Scott, had announced the cause of death as a combination of heart, liver and kidney failure and blood poisoning – Philip never did anything by halves. While Philip's body was retained in Salisbury for the autopsy, a procession of sympathisers from far and wide arrived at the house in Kew, including Percy, who had travelled down from Manchester. As the shock-waves of Philip's death travelled all over the world, more and more expressions of sympathy flooded in. I was taken, almost in a zombie-like state, to stand in a shop, crying my eyes out, while a woman fitted me with some black funeral clothes. My body started trembling from the moment I knew he had died, and continued to do so for years afterwards.

As a convenience for his English friends and fans, many of whom would have found it impossible to travel to Dublin for the funeral, it was decided to celebrate Mass, on Thursday 9th January, in the Saint Elizabeth of Portugal Church, in The Vineyard, Richmond, which he had regularly attended and where he had been married only six years previously. The church was filled to capacity and the congregation overflowed into the street.

Chris Morrison read a passage from The Bible. The attendance included Bob Geldof, his wife Paula Yates, members of bands like Motorhead and The Boomtown Rats, John Coughlan from Status Quo, and, of course, former members of Thin Lizzy. The pop group Duran Duran sent red roses. Mass was celebrated by Father Raymond Brennan, the same priest who had married Philip and Caroline. The church organist played a very emotional version of the folk tune 'Lord Of The Dance', a particular favourite of Philip's, and one which had also been played at his wedding. Sarah and Cathleen brought a personal wreath, but you could tell that they were as stunned as I was by the tragedy of it all.

After the Mass, everybody retired to the Richmond Hill Hotel for drinks and the traditional sad reminiscences about Philip and their adventures with him. It was all desperately depressing.

The most harrowing journey I have ever taken in my life was the plane trip back to Dublin for the burial on Saturday 11th January. Dennis and I and the rest of the funeral party were given an executive lounge at Heathrow Airport as we prepared to bring Philip home to Ireland for the last time. On the plane, my distress reached such black depths that I can distinctly remember feeling that I would not care if the plane crashed. At that point, I felt my life was over anyway. But then, I was struck by feelings of guilt at such a horrible thought, since there were several children on board, children who deserved the chance to grow into loving adults.

I was so completely devastated by the whole experience that I cannot even remember now whether the casket came to Glen Corr, or proceeded directly from Dublin Airport to the Requiem Mass at the Church Of The Assumption in Howth. Not that it matters – its destination was the same either way. Everywhere, the house, the church, even the roads, seemed to be teeming with people but, once again, I closed my eyes in an attempt to shut out the horrible truth. I was led about, as if I were a blind person.

I was later told that the men of Howth, dozens upon dozens of them, had taken the casket out of the hearse and passed it along at shoulder-height right up to the church, whereas normally it would have been carried by only four men – but I can't vouch for that because I was in an abyss of horror at the time and I saw virtually nothing.

The traditional Irish group, Clann Éadair, played 'The Lord Of The Dance', and a plaintive piece from *The Brendan Voyage* that soothed the spirit just a little, but it didn't last. I remember one woman mourner coming over to me and pulling at me and saying, "God help you! God help you!" and such like. She was having such an awful effect on me, although no doubt she meant well, that two friends escorted me away from her and helped me into the car for the journey to Saint Fintan's Cemetery in Sutton, a mere stone's throw from Glen Corr. The cortege passed the Royal Hotel in Howth where, only a few Sundays previously, Philip had played what must have been his last gig ever, joining members of the local band Clann Éadair for a fun session.

At the cemetery, the bitterly cold day and my inconsolable grief combined to freeze me so rigid that I could not even leave the car until a priest helped me to walk among the large, jostling crowd, some of whom had been waiting from dawn. Ten feet away from the grave, I had to stop walking. I was as close to the dead body of my son as I could possibly bear. In the long run, the fact that the funeral was attended by numerous well-known people, including former (and future) Taoiseach Charles Haughey, Bono, Adam Clayton and Larry Mullen from U2, their manager Paul McGuinness, Bob Geldof, Paula Yates, Eamon Carr from Horslips, Philip Chevron of The Pogues and, again, members of Thin Lizzy, would mean a lot to me. There were countless others from throughout the international and local music business, including musicians, managers, promoters, journalists, disc-jockeys and, most important of all, Philip's loyal fans, who had meant so much to him. But at the time, I just felt numb. Nothing could bring Philip back. That awful truth was all that mattered.

Floral tributes were sent from all over the world, from Dire Straits, Huey Lewis And The News, Gary Moore, U2, Chas And Dave and a special one from The Boomtown Rats which read, "All our love from one bunch of cowboys to another. God bless." I remember Brian Robertson's mum coming up to me at one point and, with tears streaming down her cheeks, saying, in an obvious reference to her Brian's own difficulties, "There but for the grace of God goes my son."

I remained thoroughly oblivious to the clamour that surrounded me. I was sleepwalking, almost comatose with grief. All I could see in my mind's eye were visions of my beautiful young Philip, at various stages during his life. I thought of his face when he was four years old, on the horrible morning when I had to kiss him goodbye as I left him in Dublin, with his grandmother and returned back to Manchester. I thought of him in an ill-fitting boiler suit one day when I went to visit him at work in Tonge & Taggart in Dublin. I thought of him proudly buying me a meal in that Italian restaurant in the first flush of his local celebrity. I thought of him lying on his bed in the Kew house with Sarah and Cathleen, and all three of them laughing their heads off over something silly he had said. There were moments when I genuinely believed that my head would burst open.

Unable to suppress my pain any longer, I screamed Philip's name out over the tumult of the crowd and collapsed to the ground. Big Charlie scooped me up in his arms, carried me to the car and drove straight back to Glen Corr.

THE MOURNING AFTER

"Wild one
Won't you please come home
You've been away too long, will you? . . .
How can we carry on
When you are gone, my wild one?
– from 'Wild One' by Philip Lynott

For the next two years, my life was overtaken by the most profound inner torment. I barely moved from the settee in Glen Corr upon which Charlie had set me down after whisking me away from the funeral. My weight plummeted to six and a half stone. I shook constantly and one arm developed a twitch. My hair turned white, and I became a virtual recluse.

Some people may argue that had I allowed myself to see Philip's body my grief would not have been so deep or so prolonged. When I later saw my mother's body after her death, I know I felt a certain peace, but I do not believe that I could have brought myself to see the dead body of my son.

My grief was undoubtedly compounded by the manner of his death. The passing of a loved one through some terminal disease, or in an accident, seems to have different effects on their bereaved than the presumed avoidability of a death from drugs. Add to that my confusion and disappointment stemming from my total, but ultimately hopelessly wrong, conviction that the Philip Lynott I knew would not be so weak-willed or so stupid as to allow himself to become addicted to drugs and I am left with a feeling that it was all so avoidable.

It must also be remembered that Philip and I had not lived together for any substantial period of time, and it may be that this actually added to the burden of my grief. I have a terrible, lingering sense of how much we missed out on. I could not claim to miss his physical presence from the house as such, but, although we had lived apart for long periods, there was a remarkable spiritual closeness between us. I missed his regular phone-calls. He never ended a call without saying: "I love you, Ma." And his sense of romanticism meant that he would always send me flowers or perfume on appropriate occasions. I just wish we had been together more, to share the joys of mother and son when he was growing up. I have a fierce sense of loss that continues to haunt me – but then I think it's always especially hard for a mother to bury her young son.

I couldn't bear to listen to any of Philip's music after he died. It is ironic that people often say of artists of all kinds that it is a blessing that something of their art lives on after them. But, in my case, my pain was too raw to allow me to even bear the mention of Thin Lizzy's music for a long time. I simply couldn't endure the sound of Philip's voice on the television or radio. When I passed pictures of him in the house, I would avert my eyes from his. I even requested the Thin Lizzy management office to forewarn me about any likely publicity relating to Philip or the band, so that I could specifically take precautions to avoid it. For many years, I would spend Christmases in silence, with both my television and radio switched off, rather than run the risk of hearing his voice, singing or speaking, on what was almost his anniversary.

Partly I was trying to fool myself into thinking that I had imagined it all, and that Philip was actually touring Australia or somewhere far away and that his telephone call would come at any minute. I know this probably only makes sense to me. I knew he was dead, but, because I had not seen his body, I could fantasise. How close to the borders of insanity I came I will never know, but it must have been a close shave.

In my anger, I cursed to hell and back those who either supplied his habit or stood idly by while he declined. But my anger at these people later turned to sadness and pity. Some had their own problems with drugs but have since thankfully recuperated, even if they now lower their eyes in embarrassment when we meet. Such was my anger that I was instrumental in having a former Thin Lizzy roadie, Liam Kelly, charged and convicted with supplying cocaine to Philip. He was sentenced to two years in jail in England. Eventually, however, I had to educate myself to understand that addicts, whether addicted to heroin or alcohol, tend to bond together and to lie for each other. They treat non-addicts as the enemy, foes to be ruthlessly frozen out. And I came to realise that they were more misguided than evil.

In my profound misery, Glen Corr was transformed into a silent tomb for a long time. I often lay prostrate for long periods in the house, thinking of Philip lying in his grave just a short drive away. In my unrelenting denial, I could not bring myself to visit him.

When, at last, I felt ready for that ordeal, I persuaded a friend to take me to the cemetery, where I spent some time praying for Philip's soul and tidying up his grave. I collected some smooth stones from the beach beside the house and painted them white as decorations for the grave. I also arranged for a friend called Snowy to make a white cross with Philip's name on it.

This gave his final resting place the appearance of a cowboy's grave out on the prairie, an appropriate memorial image given Philip's preoccupation with bandits, vagabonds and the romantic outlaw lifestyle. But when fans began to bring their own stones, the authorities told me that you could only have a proper regulation cross or nothing at all. I rang Caroline to persuade her that a proper stone cross should be placed at the grave. When she came to Dublin, we chose a piece of marble, but she was adamant that the headstone should not contain any of the usual sentiments which we had seen when walking around the graveyard, such as "Sadly missed by your ever-loving wife."

Although I appreciated that she wanted to be honest about their relationship, that insistence really cut deeply into me. Maybe I misinterpreted her attitude and she simply felt that kind of conventional sentimentality would be misplaced, but it seemed somehow harsh to me. I turned to Jim Fitzpatrick, the artist who had worked on several of Thin Lizzy's album covers as far back as *Vagabonds Of The Western World* in 1973, as well as *Nightlife* and *Jailbreak*, and who had been a well-loved friend of Philip's. I asked Jim, who is a dear friend to this day as well as being a neighbour, would he design a Celtic motif for the marble headstone. Rather than simply containing Philip's name, I asked him to find an appropriate Irish-language verse which could be used and which would avoid contravening Caroline's wishes. That's why the gravestone today bears the inscription in Irish "Go dtuga Dia suaimhneas dá anam, Róisín Dubh" – which roughly translates as "Sleep in peace, our Black Rose." Caroline heartily approved of these sentiments and I think Philip would have approved too. He'd have especially loved the idea of having an epitaph inscribed in Irish – Jim Fitzpatrick recalls him expressing an eloquent nationalist outlook during some of their many conversations together.

A death of this tragic kind affects every aspect of your life, even the most trivial. For a long time, I avoided my local supermarket where Philip and I used to shop, because so many people knew us both and would offer their heartfelt sympathy whenever they met me. As a result, every visit was likely to end with me in tears, shaking uncontrollably and upsetting everybody else.

Even when I learned to venture out again, I was still over-sensitive to anybody looking at me or offering me sympathy. I imagined that such people were pitying me, and looking at me as some kind of weird recluse, driven mad because of a son who died a drug addict. Which, in a way, maybe I was.

Once, in a shop in the nearby suburb of Baldoyle, I was startled to hear Philip's speaking voice, as clear as could be. For a moment, I felt he was right behind me. Dropping my purchases in horror, I put my hands over my ears. Some ladies, including one who recognised me, ran over, under the impression that I was having some kind of a fit, but I then realised that the voice I had heard was the shop's sound system pumping out a song by Philip called 'King's Call' from 1980, in which Philip does a spoken passage. As a further irony, in that song Philip tells how he consoled himself on hearing of Elvis Presley's death by going *"to the liquor store and buying a bottle of wine and a bottle of gin."*

When I recovered my composure, these good samaritans took me to a café for a recuperative cup of coffee. When one of the women explained to the waitress what had just happened, she recalled that she had once met Philip on the Dublin-Holyhead ferry, and that he had asked her for a date! The laughter which that coincidence kindled helped me over the shock of imagining I was hearing the voice of my son from beyond the grave. And in a way, that incident helped the ice to begin to thaw.

On another occasion, while visiting a friend near Gretna Green in Scotland, I had to run away from a market stall where a record player was playing 'Whisky In The Jar'. My friend explained to the lad running the stall that I was Philip Lynott's mother. Immediately, he chased after me and made a present of the record to me, saying that I could listen to it when I felt able to, which I did a long time later. Now that I can listen to Philip's music again, 'Whisky In The Jar' is a real favourite of mine. It brings back so many pleasant memories.

However, I must not pretend that I was always a big fan of all of Philip's music. As I've said, when I first saw them playing live, I could not even hear the words with the overall noise, never mind understand them. It took a while for it to grow on me since I was drawn more to artists like Frank Sinatra, Earl Bostic, The Beatles and Stan Kenton and had long kept my jazz record collection intact. Gradually, my ears became attuned to the rock sound over the years and I take some pride in being one of the few grannies of my era who love rock music.

Although it may at times have seemed otherwise, in the long run the constant stream of fans to Glen Corr was a tremendous source of comfort to me, as it made me realise how many people were genuinely touched by

Philip's music, which lived on in the hearts of so many of them. Right up to the time the Irish courts ordered me to vacate Glen Corr, I was always delighted by visits from such passionate people, all the more so as time went by. In fact, I cannot remember deliberately turning away any genuine fan who arrived on my doorstep.

It was a different matter dealing with the media, many of whom seem prepared to stoop to any level of deceit in order to trick their way into my confidence. I know that they all have a job to do in a very competitive business, but I find it sad that such people can only earn a living by being parasites on the grief of others. I can recall one Irish journalist in particular who came to meet me on the pretext of wanting to talk to me about Philip's life after the demise of Thin Lizzy. When he arrived armed with a bottle of wine, it should have aroused my suspicions. All he wanted to talk about were the sordid lies about the state of Philip's body when he was admitted to hospital.

Another journalist wormed his way into my hospitality through a female acquaintance who phoned me completely out of the blue after I had not heard from her for over a decade. These people are very sad cases, I suppose. Fortunately, there are many others in the media who are courteous and civil and honest and I will always try to accommodate them whenever I can.

The cases full of mail received from fans from all over the world helped me to keep whatever problems I had with the media in perspective, but I have to admit that I could have done with secretarial help – some of the mail remained unopened for up to five years because I found it too painful to confront the loss of one who was loved by so many.

Those were dark days but Caroline, Sarah and Cathleen often came over and their company helped me too. Caroline sometimes stayed at Adam Clayton's house in Rathfarnham. The girls were not having an easy time dealing with the aftermath of their father's death either. Sarah once got into a frightful state in London and could not stop crying. Caroline asked me to come over to help comfort her. Part of Sarah's problem, I discovered when we met, was her fear of having another father because Caroline was then dating a man and she could not bear to see his arms around Caroline. When I explained this to Caroline and her boyfriend, they understood Sarah's hurt. But inevitably, it would be necessary for Sarah to accept Caroline's needs too.

I don't want this to turn into a litany, but I was also blessed at Glen Corr by the close proximity of some truly marvellous friends, especially Dennis, of course, but also Helen Ruttle, who would come and talk to me for ages about all kinds of stuff that used to take my mind off my own grieving. The comfort I drew from the friendship of people like Graham Cohen, Dympna McKenna, Maeve Curtis' mother Trish McMahon and the entire McMahon family, and my own family, helped me enormously to come through what were very difficult times indeed. In some cases, it was enough to get a phone-call from a friendly voice or to meet for a cup of coffee with someone who I felt understood my predicament and could lend a sympathetic ear. But in truth, my awakening from this grief-torn world only began when I became interested again in what people like Helen were doing in their own lives and with the realisation that, ultimately, others had experiences as wounding, if not even more so, than mine. Life, I slowly but surely realised, goes on, no matter what.

One cold day, walking along the crisp grass in the cemetery after visiting Philip's grave, I encountered a woman engrossed in cleaning a gravestone. I quietly read the details on the stone which related the deaths of three young people in the fire that ravaged the Stardust Disco in Dublin's Artane on St Valentine's Night, 1981, claiming a total of forty-eight lives. Looking at her ice-blue hands, and feeling a wave of simple ordinary human sympathy, the realisation suddenly dawned that this woman had lost not one but *three* of her offspring. I dropped to the ground beside her, took her cloth, gave her a hug and started polishing the headstone. When that was done, I introduced myself and we stood there by the grave, talking. It was an opportunity for me to confide in someone who would understand the pain I was feeling. But, more importantly, it gave me the chance to listen to someone who had herself suffered immeasurably. What she told me was a story of savage, cruel misfortune that was utterly heartbreaking in its scale and finality.

So, I was not the first or only mother to have lost a beloved son. I slowly discovered that this cemetery, which I had subconsciously assumed was for old people who had lived out their lives, was actually packed with the graves of dozens of young people, not just Philip Lynott. I gradually began to understand that I had not been singled out for some malignant fate – and I realised that it was unworthy simply to feel sorry for myself when there is tragedy all around.

Somehow, the story got about that I had begun visiting Philip's grave every day and this was blown up into something heroic, but the truth is that I have to drive past the cemetery every day and it's no big deal to stop off. Sometimes, I find the car almost automatically turning into the parking area. I go now because I like to think! What it does do, however, is bring you closer to other people who are grieving and in pain – and in that way, I suppose it is a humbling experience.

During one visit, I happened upon one of the cemetery workers who was in considerable distress. This was a man whom one would expect to be hardened to tragedies, yet he was weeping uncontrollably, having witnessed the most harrowing funeral of a 12-year-old girl killed by a cowardly hit-and-run driver. He took me around to her grave which was covered in teddy-bears and flowers and heartbreaking messages. It was a devastating sight. Another day I met a man praying at the graveside of his son who had hanged himself a fortnight before. And on another sombre occasion, I arrived at the graveyard unwittingly at the same time as the funeral of a young woman, who had been murdered in the Dublin Mountains.

Such encounters with reality helped me to put my own situation into perspective and gave me the will to live again. Sometimes, when I'm laying flowers on Philip's grave, I imagine him saying, "Ah, Ma don't be smothering me with flowers, sure I'm a Rocker." It makes me aware of other graves that might have greater need of a few flowers. I admit now that I had become very selfish and self-centred in my misery, thinking "Oh me! Why me!" and so on, as if I should be exempt from the normal difficulties of life. My encounters with the grief of others cured me of such self-indulgence and helped me face back out into the world. It also freed me and, I think, enabled me to forgive all of Philip's associates, against whom I used to rail so violently. I had harboured a vicious anger in my heart against the suppliers of his drugs and the so-called friends who did nothing to alleviate his plight. I had kept that anger hidden, but my rage now melted away, or most of it anyway.

While reading about the lives of Elvis Presley, Bob Marley, Jimi Hendrix and Jim Morrison, I saw many similarities between the pressures of their lives (and deaths) and Philip's. In particular, I saw how Philip's hero Jimi Hendrix had died in circumstances not dissimilar to Philip's own tragic end. All of these stars had serious and fatal drug problems of one kind or another, and learning something of their lives helped me to understand a little about some of the crazy pressures high-profile people like Philip must cope with. It also served to bring home to me the fact that there are those who believe they are actually indestructible and that they can handle virtually everything. I have a feeling that, until he was close to the end, Philip was one of those.

Different drugs have different effects on people. Looking back I now feel that certain substances made Philip aggressive, whereas he was a gentle guy at heart. Like me, he was never a great sleeper and drugs may have helped him in that regard, who knows? Hard drugs initially may have seemed to him like an adventure or a respite from the glare of the spotlight he referred to in 'Dancing In The Moonlight'. Towards the end, it is widely known that his fortunes had taken a dispiriting turn in terms of his career, and he may even have been encountering money problems. Thin

Lizzy had split and he had no record deal to compensate for his substantial investment in his new project, Grand Slam. All of this might have speeded his downward spiral or, at least, added further burdens to his existing problems.

Whatever the background details may have been, it is worth repeating, over and over again, that Philip's death was an appalling waste and a source of great pain to many people who loved him in spite of his faults – but his demise was part of life and the rest of us must carry on. Nobody, no matter how talented or how loving or how young, is safe from the ravages of death, which can overtake you at any time. This is even truer today with the drug epidemic and all the crime and violence that goes with it. Kids at parties, at school and at other gatherings are called cowards if they say 'No' to drugs, so if my adult son, a great hero to so many, could not avoid the pitfalls, what chance has a young teenager?

The drugs are available in ever-increasing quantities and no government or agency anywhere in the world seems even remotely capable of preventing their continued spread.

I don't know what the answer is, but it still hurts me when I see Philip referred to in the press as a 'junkie'. There is something squalid about the word and, in his case, it conjures up inaccurate images of someone down and out and living friendless on the streets.

I look at it differently. Surely, Philip would not, and could not, have hurt his beloved daughters, his mother, his other relations and friends unless he had been a very sick person?

Drug addicts, I believe, are sick people and, just as society in recent decades has come to understand that alcoholism is an illness, we must do likewise regarding those afflicted with other addictions, bearing in mind that heroin, and perhaps cocaine, are even more lethal than alcohol, when bought on the black market, from drug dealers, with all the attendant risks of contamination and over-dosing.

At first, in trying to avoid coming to terms with the manner of Philip's death, I had hidden myself away, but now I can cope with it and perhaps use my experience to help prevent other mothers and sons from going through the hell I suffered. And, more to the point, the hell that Philip himself must have suffered.

Inevitably, there were issues which needed to be resolved in Philip's affairs, following his death. Among these, the most contentious related to the house in Glen Corr, which had such powerful associations with Philip for me, and where I lived in the aftermath of his death. However, Caroline felt that this house should be sold – an attitude with which I just couldn't agree. A dispute developed and, as a result, Caroline began to discourage meetings between me and Sarah and Cathleen. This hurt me deeply, especially because it was I who had been there for her during the births of both children, whom I truly love. That was what I did, making myself available as a support and occasional surrogate mother when the going got tough or people needed me.

In the end, the differences were bitter and could only be settled by going to court.

One of the reasons I was prepared to go this far to try to prevent Caroline taking possession of Glen Corr, and then selling it, was that I knew Philip had bought the house as a residence for Sarah and Cathleen so that they could settle in Ireland. The way I saw it, it was always meant to be their house. Both were born in Ireland, at Philip's insistence. It was their childhood home. I distinctly recall Sarah turning to me one day and saying, "I love this house." The way I saw it, in a few years, the girls could have been given the opportunity to make their own decisions. I couldn't see the need to move on selling the house sooner.

Some people wrongly assume that, as his mother, I must somehow benefit from the sales of Philip's records – but there's absolutely no reason why I should. Sometimes it seems that his music is played on the radio in Ireland now more than ever before, but all that money goes to his legal next of kin, and rightly so. I do not, and never did, want any of that money for myself. I know that Caroline is a good mother who loves her children, but I wanted to do whatever I could to ensure that Philip's daughters would be taken care of to the greatest extent possible, and that's the only reason I asked the court that I be allowed to remain in Glen Corr until they were able to make their own minds up. I was definitely not claiming the house for myself, and I do not want people, no matter how well-intentioned, feeling I lost it in the courts. Since I have always believed in obeying the law, there was no option for me other than to vacate Glen Corr, painful though that experience was to become.

Others thought this was a scandalous outcome, and told me so, not only because of the possibility that Sarah and Cathleen might be deprived of the chance to own the house their father had bought for them to grow up in, but also because the house had, over the years since Philip's death, become the primary focal point for his fans. Without being in the least ghoulish, it had virtually become an unofficial Philip Lynott museum. Indeed, one of the rooms was often described by visitors as a veritable shrine to Philip, so full was it of artefacts and mementos relating to various aspects of his life and career. Even if, personally, I find that description a little fanciful, it is not totally off the mark.

Looking back, it is easy to see that his busy career left Philip virtually no time in which to enjoy his marriage or fatherhood and the normal ups and downs of ordinary life. In the same way, he never had a proper chance to enjoy Glen Corr and I retain a very fond memory of him walking around the rear garden and saying, "Imagine, Ma, I own all this. Isn't it lovely?"

Philip loved the house, and perhaps, if his life had not taken the tragic turn it did, he would have settled down there with his family for the rest of his natural life. And this story, if told at all, would have had a genuinely happy ending.

DEATH IS NOT THE END

"If you see my mother
Please give her all my love
For she has a heart of gold there
As good as God above
If you see my mother
Tell her I'm keeping fine
Tell her that I love her
And I'll try to write sometime."
– from 'Philomena' by Philip Lynott.

It has indeed been claimed about many artists in different fields that something of them lives on in their art beyond death. In that sense, it is gratifying to know that, through their recordings, Philip and Thin Lizzy are still bringing happiness and pleasure to people. Equally, it is not every mother whose son can leave behind a piece of music with such loving sentiments as are contained in the song 'Philomena'. Philip wrote this song especially for me and recorded it on his birthday, in 1974, for inclusion on the *Nightlife* album. In the middle of a hard rock album, it's a lovely moment of romanticism.

Philip loved writing songs about real people, particularly people who were important in his life. The *Nightlife* album, for instance, also features a song called 'Frankie Carroll' which is about Frank Murray, Thin Lizzy's tour manager, and Ted Carroll, their manager before the two Chrises took command. He also wrote lovely songs for both of his daughters, Sarah and Cathleen. Such tributes were Philip's way of telling his friends and of course his children, how much they meant to him. For me, 'Philomena' is a monument not just to Philip's poetic talent and his creativity but also to his ability to love – and I treasure it greatly.

Another of Philip's friends, Smiley Bolger, who has been wrongly criticised and unfairly maligned over the years, has been more active than anyone in keeping Philip's memory alive, particularly through the *Ode To A Black Man* records and tapes he has issued, and through his annual Vibe For Philo concert which has taken place on the anniversary of his death every year since 1987. Some malicious individuals put round the story that Smiley was personally making capital out of these projects, but after each event he comes to my house and goes through his bills scrupulously, accounting for every penny of the income and expenditure. And the gigs are always genuinely warm and moving occasions.

To hear young bands, some of whose members may not have even been born when the band was at its peak, performing Thin Lizzy music with energy and dedication, lifts my heart. Well-known singers like Elvis Costello, Sinéad O'Connor, Joe Elliott from Def Leppard and Philip Chevron of The Pogues, have all given of their time to the various remembrance projects, at Smiley's prompting.

And all the time, the dedication to Philip's memory and his art is growing. Thanks to Smiley's efforts in showing the way, there are now annual commemorative concerts in countries as far apart as Sweden and Japan. In many ways, Smiley is like me in that he believes in speaking the truth forthrightly to people he trusts. Although this has led to us having many a dispute over the years, I love him dearly and will not hear anyone say a harsh word against him. Without his voluntary and selfless efforts, Philip's memory would certainly not be as prominently cherished around the world as it is today.

The way I feel now, the more of this, the better. I've come a long way from the time when I wanted to run away from images of Philip. Consequently, it was another source of great pride to me when Smithwicks and *Hot Press* asked for my approval for the introduction of

The Philip Lynott New Band Award as part of the annual *Hot Press* Music Critics Awards. The idea was suggested to me by Jackie Hayden of *Hot Press*, who has also helped me to write this book, and by Paul Keeley, who works with the Guinness Group. They had decided to honour Philip in this way because he had a reputation for helping young bands who may not have had the money for demos or the knowledge of how to go about making a good studio recording. In this way, he had been an enormous help to many bands, including the Howth band Clann Éadair on whose single, 'Tribute To Sandy Denny', he sang in 1984. He also produced four singles for the Dublin-based band Auto Dá Fé in the early 1980s.

The fact that Paul Keeley shared the same surname as Dennis must have been a good omen and I agreed to endorse their proposal. I still think it is a brilliant way of commemorating Philip's name in a very practical sense. That said, attending the awards ceremony was something of a trial the first year because it was one of the only occasions I had been among young rock people since my son's death, and seeing long-legged men with long hair, but with no sign of Philip among them, made me feel lost and emotional. When I was making my small speech from the stage, I started to stammer and lose my way. As I looked down from the stage through misting eyes, I caught a glimpse of a young chap in the audience looking back at me with tears rolling down his cheeks. That helped me to carry on and, eventually, I got through the speech.

Despite my initial stagefright, however, I have been delighted to present the award every year since its inauguration and to meet so many well-wishers in the media and among the music community.

The setting up of the Róisín Dubh Trust was another boost for my morale, not only because it spreads the difficulty of dealing with the growing number of activities related to Philip, but because of the calibre of the people who agreed to give of their time to serve, without any kind of financial remuneration, on the committee. In particular, I should express my appreciation to Ailish Courtney-Baldwin, who was a tower of strength to me throughout the ordeal of my court battle over Glen Corr.

Sometimes her sense of outrage over what was happening exceeded my own and without her I am not sure if I would have found the energy to fight to the end.

Those are essential practical concerns but there have been other events which are way beyond my understanding, but which offer a degree of hope to all of us who have some spiritual aspect to our nature. Some time after Philip's death, Caroline took Sarah and Cathleen to a small cottage in Cornwall for a much-needed break. Just after she had settled into her room, Cathleen ran out to Caroline saying, "Daddy's in the cupboard in my room and he says he's going to mind us no matter where we go." She repeated this excitedly several times as if she were totally convinced of what she had seen. The point is not necessarily that it happened, but that the little girl believed that it did.

Curiously, there have been other, similar, incidents which at least confirm the powerful grip that the presence of someone like Philip holds on people's hearts, their minds and their imaginations. While I was going through a very bad time, Jim Fitzpatrick called to Glen Corr and told me he had a strange story to recount, but he was a bit hesitant because he feared it might be upsetting for me. I insisted that he go ahead and he then proceeded to tell me that Philip had appeared to him in New York, not once but on two separate occasions. Subsequent to that, I heard of a young male fan in Liverpool who had written to the *Liverpool Echo* to say that a vision of Philip had appeared before him.

In a similar vein, Darren Wharton, who had joined Thin Lizzy on keyboards for the *Chinatown* and *Renegade* albums, told me in the presence of a close friend of mine that Philip had appeared to his wife and himself simultaneously, shortly after they had moved into a new house. When he was telling me this, his wife was five months pregnant. My first response was to blurt out, "I wish he'd appear to me!" – though in truth, I did not, and do not, really wish that to happen. Nevertheless, I did wonder aloud to the company whether her baby might be born on Philip's birthday. I was back in Dublin when Darren phoned on 20th August 1990, Philip's birthday, to say that his wife had given birth that very day. He named his son Daniel Parris, the second name as his personal tribute to Philip. I can never explain fully how much a genuine gesture like that means to me.

Then, when I was in Sweden in 1993 for a birthday tribute concert, a young girl told me that Philip had appeared to her and instructed her to tell me that he was at peace and was happy. Do I think she was really a conduit for Philip to pass a message to me? I suppose the real point is that it made both of us feel just a little bit better. Personally, I have never encountered such inexplicable events in my own life, and I have never shown any interest in spiritualism or any related subject, so I can offer no explanation – yet those involved have little to gain in risking being branded as gullible or eccentric by revealing these occurrences to a cynical world. I have learned to keep an open mind on the revelations of others, whereas there was certainly a time when I might have belittled such experiences.

Of course, Philip has featured in my dreams on many occasions. There was one in particular, which recurred, in which I enter a room where there lies a newborn baby covered up in a cot. The phone rings and I hear Philip's voice on the line saying, "I'm still alive, come on around to see me." I run frantically around the house looking for him, and when I look into the cot it's him exactly as he was as a baby. The disappointment I feel on waking up after such dreams is impossible to express.

There have been other mysteries and somewhat strange coincidences. An elderly couple called at Glen Corr one day. As a child, the husband, whose mother was a previous owner of the house, had planted all the roses that had grown so decorously in the back garden. Over a cup of tea, I discovered that they were living in Salisbury, where Philip had died. They also told me that their son had gone to view a house for sale in Bath not realising that Philip's ex-wife owned it. About a year later, I was visited by their two beautiful daughters, one of whom had taken a teaching post in Malahide, a small harbour village not much further north along the coast from Howth. I suppose these kinds of incidents happen all the time, but they take on an added resonance when someone has died.

Initially, when people told me how lucky I was to have Philip's musical legacy as a permanent memento of him, I just thought, "None of that matters. None of it can replace the person I loved so much. I'd much rather have him alive." But, later, I began to appreciate and study that legacy, and it has become a source of great comfort to me. Similar comments have been made about the comfort the grand-children must be to me, but, much as I love them dearly, they cannot replace Philip in my life. I can only compare the pain of a mother losing a child in death to what I imagine to be the pain of being tortured. In crude terms, Philip's death was akin to someone delivering a vicious blow to my head and the ensuing numbness has taken years to diminish.

Of course, it helps that so many love his music, but I would give it all up, willingly and instantly, just to have him back in my life.

FRIENDS, RELATIONS AND ACQUAINTANCES

There was, I think, less of the big-headedness around Thin Lizzy that you expect from rock bands and famous people generally. As their success grew, it was like one enormous bandwagon as Philip invited more and more of his friends to climb on board. As most of the various members and crew who paraded through the ranks of Thin Lizzy were Irish anyway, they made a tight family – at least it seemed that way most of the time when I was around.

Inevitably, I was particularly fond of Brian Downey, a fundamentally decent, trustworthy and considerate man. An only child born to his parents late in their lives, Brian drummed with Philip's first serious band, The Black Eagles. In fact, I've known Brian since he was twelve years of age and often visited his mum and dad in Crumlin. Brian lives in Dublin and we are still very close. I doubt if a serious cross word has ever passed between us.

But there were other great characters and friends whom Philip thought the world of – and who thought the world of Philip. I always liked Midge Ure, who replaced Gary Moore in the band for a while before Snowy White joined, and I always enjoyed meeting and talking to both Scott Gorham and Brian Robertson, the twin guitar heroes of the albums from *Fighting* on. They played on *Live and Dangerous*, which many people consider the definitive Thin Lizzy album, and I always thought that they struck a great balance visually as well as musically.

Darren Wharton, who played with Thin Lizzy during the latter part of their career, is another former member with whom I have kept up contact over the years, and I have also met his family. John Sykes, who joined

Lizzy from the Tygers Of Pan Tang in the early 1980s, always sends me flowers and books on my birthday and at Christmas, because he knew how much I appreciated Philip doing likewise on such occasions.

I know that this might seem like a roll call, but I do want the people who have been good to me – and who were good to Philip – to know that what they gave along the way was appreciated.

Another great pal was Frank Murray, who worked with Philip from the early days and who, along with his wife Ferga, spent their honeymoon with us in Ibiza. Philip was always very loyal to those who were his friends or who had been supportive of the band in the past. People like Studs, who became a roadie with Lizzy after his father took him to see the band in Belfast, and who still keeps in touch, and like Gus Curtis, who was always close to Philip. And like Big Charlie McLennan, who was with him in his final hours. In many ways, these backroom workers are the unsung heroes of rock'n'roll and I want to pay tribute to them here.

In 1993, I was delighted to renew my acquaintance with Thin Lizzy's early guitarist Eric Bell when I visited Sweden for a celebration of Thin Lizzy's music in an event inspired by Smiley Bolger's annual Vibe For Philo. It was Eric's departure from the band in 1973 that seemed to be to be their first major setback. He was replaced temporarily by Gary Moore, before a more permanent arrangement was made with Brian Robertson and Scott Gorham. It's great to know that Eric is still trucking away, and playing as well as ever by all accounts!

The only person in the Lizzy camp to whom I never became close was Gary Moore. It might have been our different personalities, but we did not hit it off in the same way as I did with the others. Matters were not helped by an incident which occurred when Gary brought a bizarre girl-friend to the Clifton Grange. During the course of the day, the girl got very drunk and – quite unashamedly, I thought – made a pass at Philip. She was quite young and was perhaps a little naive. She became incensed when I told her that she was the kind of woman who causes bands to split up. I think Gary innocently suspected that Philip was trying something on with her and the incident caused "bad vibes" between us.

I wanted to report the incident to the band management but Philip, ever the diplomat, preferred not to upset Gary, whose guitar-playing he really admired. When Gary later abandoned Lizzy during a crucial tour of America in 1979, he certainly earned no credit in my eyes, jeopardising everybody's livelihood after all the work and preparation that had gone into putting a world tour together. Nevertheless, I'm sure that Gary has his side of the story too – he would hardly have taken such a drastic step unless there were some deep divisions within the band.

I am aware, too, that some people who shall remain nameless had long been endeavouring to engineer a personal rift between Philip and Gary. As I understand it, he was constantly being needled about the fact that he was playing "second fiddle" to Philip Lynott. The common knowledge is that there were ego clashes between the pair of them, and I doubt that Philip was entirely innocent in that department. That said, he was the leader of Thin Lizzy and its driving force – and to climb on board at all implied an acceptance of that.

Of course, Gary is a very talented man in his own right, as even a single listen to his beautiful solo on 'Still In Love With You' on the 1973 album *Nightlife* can testify. He was perfectly entitled to quit the band if he no longer felt fulfilled by the music they were making, although perhaps his timing could have been more considerate! Still, I bear him no ill-will and I am glad he has been so successful as a solo artist and that he and Philip, despite their numerous personal differences, could work together on Gary's solo album, *Back On The Streets*, in 1978. Brian Downey also played drums on that album, further proof that no matter what transpires at times to cause the occasional rift, musicians who have been together a long time form a bond which is almost permanent. Philip sang on Gary's excellent hit single, 'Parisienne Walkways', in 1979 and they both sang on Gary's anti-war song 'Out In The Fields' in 1985. Philip attended Gary's wedding in Lincolnshire, in 1985, and I believe he even did a couple of songs for the guests – so you could say that they really were compadres to the end.

Contrary to popular belief, it is only in recent times that I have got to know Brush Shiels on a personal level. More than almost anybody else, his name is often linked with Philip's, because of their connection stretching back to the early days of Skid Row. Brush is outspoken and opinionated, but I always respect someone who is open and honest about their feelings. It might mean you have the occasional falling-out, but it is also often easier to sort out your disagreements afterwards. In 1986, Brush released a song he had written called 'Old Pal' and I think that song expressed his true feelings about Philip in a way that no conversation could.

Finally, it is worth saying that Philip's successful career was extremely important in helping to put the early days of conflict between me and my family behind us. Over the years, I was able to enjoy a really deep relationship with my sisters Josephine, Betty, Marian and Irene, my brothers John, Timmy and Peter, as well as my two nephews Ronnie and Reggie. In time, they all became big fans of Thin Lizzy and we enjoyed many memorable nights at gigs together. We all, I suppose, have come a long way.

"Schoolboy eyes
would stare in innocent fun
never told no lies
he loved Sarah."
– from 'Sarah' by Philip Lynott.

Philip Lynott composed two songs with the title 'Sarah'. While the 1979 'Sarah', on the *Black Rose* album, obviously expresses his delight at the birth of his first daughter, it is generally accepted that an earlier song called 'Sarah', quoted from above and recorded on the 1972 album *Shades*

Of a Blue Orphanage, is about my mother, after whom he named his daughter.

She was a lovely, strong, generous woman and she got a great thrill out of having a pop song named after her. But that song is important in that it serves as a permanent and fitting reminder of just how important a place she occupied in Philip's thoughts and in his life. He never ever forgot the sacrifices she had made in order to help us both at a particularly difficult time in our lives. Nor did I.

I was always grateful to her for her charitable and courageous move in taking Philip under her wing when his presence was certain to be a source of unpleasant gossip, not to mention a burden on her energies, patience and what little finances she had. When she was reaching the end of her life, I went out of my way to ensure that she did not have to enter a home and live out her remaining days without friends or family. It was the least I could do to return just a small part of the enormous favour she had done both Philip and I.

I can vividly remember her being in Glen Corr with me. One day as I was carrying her to the bathroom in my arms, she looked at me and said, "You're a really wonderful person." The reality was that it was she who had been so wonderful to me, but I will treasure her words and her unselfishness till the day I die.

In that sense, while this book is about Philip Lynott and Philomena Lynott, in the end – like Philip's life – it is a tribute to the ordinary decent Dublin woman who truly knew what it was to give everything.

I can say that with absolute confidence, knowing that it's the way Philip would want it.

POSTSCRIPT

This book would not have been possible were it not for the generous co-operation of the following people:

Jackie Hayden, who had the difficult task of interviewing me about sometimes painful memories and intimate aspects of my life. This, he always did with professional firmness, kindness and courtesy. Without him, I would not have been able to delve so deeply into my own thoughts and feelings. In some ways, his probing questioning helped me to face up to the reality of my life and Philip's.

Niall Stokes for his time in carefully editing the text and selecting the photographs.

Smiley Bolger and Adam Winstanley for painstakingly proof-reading the first draft and offering so many helpful suggestions and criticisms.

During the lowest periods of my grieving for Philip, I was extremely fortunate to have a number of dear friends in England who always made me welcome in their homes and took very good care of me. In this regard I owe an enormous debt to Mrs. Joan Schiavo and her family, Angela and her daughter Kim Tricket, Rita and Jack Rowles and my close friend June Ricci.

And of course there are the fans of Philip and of Thin Lizzy all over the world, whose dedication has inspired me – thank you.

In some cases I have altered the names of individuals in order to protect their privacy.

I have tried to check as many of the facts of my story as possible. However, I hope the reader will understand if either defective memory or the trauma of certain events have lead to the occasional lapse of accuracy.

Finally, although the above individuals have been of tremendous assistance, the thoughts and views contained in this book are mine alone. I express them not with the purpose of boosting my ego or of blaming others but simply to express the truth as I see it. I accept that some will not agree with some of my conclusions, but I can only tell my story the way I see it, feel it and lived it.

Philomena Lynott,
Dublin 1995

THIN LIZZY DISCOGRAPHY 1970-1986

SINGLES AND EPS

1970   The Farmer/I Need You

1971   NEW DAY EP Dublin/Remembering Part 2/Old Moon
        Madness/Things Ain't Working Out Down On The Farm

1972   Whisky In The Jar/Black Boys On The Corner

1973   Randolph's Tango/Broken Dreams
        The Rocker/Here I Go Again

1974   Little Darlin'/Buffalo Girl
        Philomena/Sha La La

1975   Rosalie/Half Caste
        Wild One/For Those Who Love To Live

1976   The Boys Are Back In Town/Emerald
        Jailbreak/Running Back
        Don't Believe A Word/Old Flame
        Dancing In The Moonlight/Bad Reputation

1978   Whisky In The Jar/Vagabond Of The Western World/Sitamoia
        Rosalie/Cowgirl's Song medley/Me And The Boys

1979   Waiting For An Alibi/With Love
        Do Anything You Want To/Just The Two Of Us
        Things Ain't Working Out Down On The Farm/The Rocker/
        Little Darlin'
        Sarah/Got To Give It Up

1980   Chinatown/Sugar Blues
        Killer On The Loose/Don't Play Around (also available in a pack
        with Got To Give It Up/Chinatown)

1981   Are You Ready/Dear Miss Lonely Heart/Bad Reputation (also avail able with Opium Trail)

Song For Jimmy (flexidisc)

Trouble Boys/Memory Pain

Hollywood (Down On Your Luck)/The Pressure Will Blow

1983 Cold Sweat/Bad Habits also available with Angel Of Death/Don't Believe A Word

Thunder And Lightning/Still In Love With You

The Sun Goes Down/Baby Please Don't Go

Whisky In The Jar/The Rocker

1985 Dancing In The Moonlight/Don't Believe A Word

ALBUMS

1971 Thin Lizzy

1972 Shades Of A Blue Orphanage

1973 Vagabonds Of The Western World

1974 Night Life

1975 Fighting

1976 Jailbreak

Remembering Part One (compilation)

Johnny The Fox

1977 Bad Reputation

1978 Live And Dangerous (double album)

1979 Black Rose-A Rock Legend

The Continuing Saga Of The Ageing Orphans (compilation)

1980 Chinatown

1981 The Adventures Of Thin Lizzy (compilation)

Renegade

Rockers (compilation)

1983 Thunder And Lightning

Lizzy Killers (previously released as The Adventures Of Thin Lizzy)

Life (double album-live)

The Boys Are Back In Town (compilation)
1984   Whisky In The Jar (double cassette compilation)
1985   The Collection (compilation)
1994   The Peel Sessions (live recordings from 1972-1977)

PHILIP LYNOTT SOLO 1980-1985

SINGLES

1980   Dear Miss Lonely Hearts/Solo In Soho
        King's Call/Ode To A Black Man
1981   Yellow Pearl/Girls
1982   Together/Somebody Else's Dream
        Old Town/Beat Of The Drum
1985   Nineteen/Nineteen (Dub Mix) also available with A Night In The
        Life Of A Blues Singer

ALBUMS

1980   Solo In Soho
1982   The Philip Lynott Album

WHERE TO WRITE:

BLACK ROSE-THE THIN LIZZY MAGAZINE,
c/o Adam C Winstanley,
1 Parson Court, Maynooth,
County Kildare,
Ireland.

THE ROISIN DUBH TRUST,
White Horses,
Sutton,
Co Dublin.

THE THIN LIZZY SUPPORTERS CLUB,
P.O. Box 4024,
Tooting,
London SW17 7EN.

HOT PRESS MAGAZINE,
13 Trinity Street,
Dublin 2.

ALSO AVAILABLE FROM HOT PRESS BOOKS.

U2: THREE CHORDS AND THE TRUTH
Edited by Niall Stokes

Critical, entertaining, comprehensive and revealing, *U2: Three Chords And The Truth* never misses a beat as it brings you, in words and pictures, a complete portrait of U2 in the process of becoming a legend.
Price: £8.95

THEY ARE OF IRELAND
by Declan Lynch

They Are Of Ireland is a hilarious who's who of famous Irish characters — and chancers — from the worlds of politics, sport, religion, the Arts, entertainment and the media. Written by Declan Lynch, one of the major new Irish literary talents of the '90s, this is one of those rare events — a book of comic writing that actually makes you laugh out loud.
Price: £7.99

U2: Three Chords And The Truth and *They Are Of Ireland* are available from Hot Press, 13 Trinity St. Dublin 2. Trade enquiries Tel: (01) 6795077 or Fax: (01) 6795097. Mail order, send cheques/POs or credit card details for £8.95 and £7.99 respectively (incl. p & p) to the above address.

PHILOMENA LYNOTT, was born in Dublin in 1930. Affectionately known as Phyllis, she left Dublin to study nursing in Birmingham — a career which she was unable to pursue when she became pregnant with her one and only son, Philip Lynott. She owned and managed the legendary Clifton Grange Hotel in Manchester for many years. In the wake of her son Philip's success with Thin Lizzy, she returned to Ireland to establish a business in Dublin with him. She has remained in Dublin since his tragic death in 1986. This is her first book.

JACKIE HAYDEN began working in the music industry as Promotions Manager for Polydor Ireland in the late '60s. He also played drums in local bands and produced records by numerous local artists. From 1972 to 1980 he was Marketing Manager with CBS Ireland, where he signed U2 to their first record deal – he has often been referred to as the man who discovered U2. He is now General Manager and a director of Hot Press magazine and runs his own music industry consultancy company Words & Music Ltd.

A founder member of the Jobs In Music Campaign, in 1995 he was appointed to the government Task Force on the Irish music industry, chairing the Committee on the International Marketing of Irish Music. As a journalist he has written for numerous publications, including the Sunday Times and Hot Press. He was responsible for inaugurating the Heineken-Hot Press Music Critics Awards. In 1993 he was given a Special Irish Music Industry Award by a panel drawn from the Irish media.

Since 1977, HOT PRESS has established a reputation as Ireland's most lively and controversial magazine - as well as one of the world's most influential music publications.

With its roots in rock'n'roll, the fortnightly HOT PRESS has become a forum for some of the finest journalism covering contemporary music, plus the best English-language writing available in print on current affairs, cinema, sport, fashion, sex, leisure and the environment. Hot Press interviews with leading politicians, personalities and stars have received widespread national and international coverage. Past contributors have included Bono and Adam Clayton (U2), Elvis Costello, Philip Chevron (The Pogues), Enya, Hugh Cornwell (The Stranglers), Bob Geldof, Tom Dunne (Something Happens) and Noel Redding (ex-Jimi Hendrix Experience).

SUBSCRIBE NOW AND GET A FREE CD!